GET THE JOB YOU WANT IN THIRTY DAYS

Berkley Books by Gary Joseph Grappo

GET THE JOB YOU WANT IN THIRTY DAYS
THE TOP 10 CAREER STRATEGIES FOR THE YEAR 2000 AND BEYOND
THE TOP 10 FEARS OF JOB SEEKERS

GET THE JOB YOU WANT IN THIRTY DAYS

Revised and Updated

GARY JOSEPH GRAPPO

BERKLEY BOOKS, NEW YORK

This book is an original publication of The Berkley Publishing Group.

GET THE JOB YOU WANT IN THIRTY DAYS

A Berkley Book / published by arrangement with
the author

PRINTING HISTORY
Berkley trade paperback edition / March 1994
Berkley revised trade paperback edition / October 1997

The Putnam Berkley World Wide Web site address is
http://www.berkley.com

ISBN: 0-425-16061-0

BERKLEY®
Berkley Books are published by The Berkley Publishing Group,
a member of Penguin Putnam Inc.,
200 Madison Avenue, New York, New York 10016.
BERKLEY and the ''B'' design
are trademarks belonging to Berkley Publishing Corporation.

PRINTED IN THE UNITED STATES OF AMERICA

10 9 8 7 6 5 4 3 2 1

TO MY PARENTS—
who taught me never to say "I can't"

TO MY SISTERS—
who helped me believe "I can"

TO TIM—
friend and colleague

And in memory of my brother,
JAMES PAUL GRAPPO, JR.,
who recently began to live.

SPECIAL ACKNOWLEDGMENTS

Leonard Evans

Denis Waitley

Brian Tracy

CONTENTS

CHARTS AND EXERCISES

GET THE JOB
YOU WANT IN
THIRTY DAYS

INTRODUCTION

In *Get the Job You Want in Thirty Days*, Gary Joseph Grappo has formulated a daily action plan for you. This plan, when properly executed, virtually guarantees you will get a job in thirty days or less. The key to achieving your objective is to utilize Mr. Grappo's plan. If you follow this plan daily, you will realize your goal.

Gary Joseph Grappo is founder and former president of CareerEdge, leaders of career seminars for major colleges and universities and job fairs nationwide. He is the author of *The Top 10 Fears of Job Seekers* and *The Top 10 Career Strategies for Making a Living in the Year 2000 and Beyond*, contributing writer to *The Wall Street Journal's National Business Employment Weekly*, and coauthor of the career bestseller *How to Write Better Résumés*.

Get the Job You Want in Thirty Days is the result of years of expertise brought to you in an easy-to-follow system.

Along with learning how to effectively utilize your daily activity planner, you will discover:

1. Why having defined goals is important and how you can clearly define your own goals

2. The importance of a positive attitude and how to maintain that attitude even when the going gets tough

3. How to create successful résumés and cover letters that result in interviews and how to utilize the best of today's technology to create them

4. Effective ways to play the "numbers game" through creative face-to-face networking as well as how to utilize the Internet's on-line resources

5. What you should and should not do at an interview

6. The importance of follow-up and how to use it effectively

FOREWORD

Someone once said, "Necessity is the mother of invention." Possibly someone should also have said, "Invention is the process by which we increase the quality of life not only for ourselves but also for others."

Helping yourself before taking on the awesome task of helping others is often a difficult lesson to learn. It's the minor lessons in life that in time turn out to be profound, life-changing principles. Master them and we are compelled to tell the world.

Writing this book results first and foremost from being a job seeker. This system, like most inventions, is the result of personal trial and error. It is also the result of a sincere desire to help others as a professional with many years of experience in the human resources field.

I do not separate my professional and personal life. The philosophy for both is the law of cause and effect, which can be stated in a variety of ways:

For every action, there is a reaction.

Whatever you sow, so shall you reap.

Give and it will be given to you.

This book not only makes good business sense, but also is based upon very fundamental principles for successful living. It searches for ears that hear and eyes that see. The risk remains, however, that after all is said and done, it may only be ink on paper. Even so, readers who thirst for success in all that they do will take this book and make it their success.

Success! Yes, success!

HOW TO USE THIS BOOK

It is important that you read this book from front to back. If chapters are read out of sequence, an important building process is thwarted. There are thirty key concepts that depend on the same principles utilized by home builders and bricklayers: The foundation must be solid. The full significance of the thirty key concepts will be realized when each previous step is understood, accepted, and acted upon. The first two chapters are particularly essential to the building process as they are not only the foundation but also the roots.

After reading the book in its entirety, I encourage you to make daily use of the activity planner. Besides giving you an action plan, it also contains a quick reference of the thirty key concepts. The quick reference is provided to help you reduce pages of information to key essentials that, in turn, should be memorized and acted upon. With these tools, nothing can stop you.

1

GOAL-SETTING PRELIMINARIES

Right out of college I had the fortunate experience, which I will share in more detail later, of meeting an elderly pastor, a noted author and speaker by the name of Leonard Evans. It was he who helped me get my career off to the right start. Leonard had a way of looking you in the eye and pointedly asking the right questions. He never gave advice. His technique was to make you create your own solutions.

When I went to him seeking counsel about my career, the first questions he asked revolved around goal-setting. "What are your goals? What do you like to do?" he asked. The questions left me speechless. I must admit, I was taken by surprise. I had never thought about those things before. At that point, I had very little to say.

Leonard then provoked a reaction with his next question. "If you had your druthers—forget about money, opportunity, or the right connections—what would you be doing with your life right now?" Immediately, a lengthy discussion transpired. For the first time in my life, I was forced to clearly identify, verbalize, and write down my likes and dislikes. Through this question, the lightbulbs began to go on. The message was clear: Go after the things you like to do and the money will follow. There is a popular book out now that summarizes where Reverend Evans was leading me. The title is, *Do What You Love, the Money Will Follow*, by Marsha Sinetar.

An illustration of this is in the story of a great pioneer woman. You may remember her legend. As a child, she asked her parents for a set of paints and brushes. Her interest in painting was dismissed as costly and foolish. Instead, as a young teenager she was married off to an older gentleman, and she raised a large family. When she was a seventy-five-year-old widow, she decided to do what she had always loved: She decided to paint. Within five years, she established American primitive art as a style. She became known as Grandma Moses. After an exhibit at the Metropolitan Museum of Art and other exhibits around the nation, some of her work began to sell for over $100,000 each. The sale of one painting yielded her more money in a day than she and her husband had made in a lifetime.

Brian Tracy, in his tape series *The Science of Self-Confidence*, states that there are four possible paths for one's life. They are:

1. Things that are hard to do to and hard to learn (i.e., rebuilding automobile engines)

2. Things that are easy to learn but hard to do (i.e., carrying bricks to a construction site)

3. Things that are hard to learn but easy to do (i.e., operating a cash register)

4. Things that are easy to learn and easy to do (varies for each person)

Brian Tracy explains that the fourth item is what we ideally should be doing with our lives. These things that are so easy for us may be hard to learn and hard to do for others. Reflect a moment on the things that you learn easily and perform well. They are generally the very things that make you happy because you enjoy doing them. This type of introspection begins to uncover your ideal career path and goals.

Before beginning your job search, it is important to identify your strengths, likes, weaknesses, and dislikes. Based on this information, you will have identified the things that produce an almost religious fervor inside of you, propelling your career to success.

Before establishing goals, it is important to realize how they are achieved. After all, no one wants to set a goal that is impossible to achieve. In fact, it is the fear of failure that discourages many individuals from setting goals. These people assume that they will never fail if they never set goals. This is far from the truth. What is worse than failure? Never trying! Making no goals and no decisions is true failure. Otherwise, there are no failures in life, just learning experiences.

When properly motivated, we can attain our goals. As a child, you may remember being promised an ice cream bar or a toy if you would behave and not embarrass everyone at a family outing. This motivational reward system certainly had its merits. It's also good psychology, according to Pavlov and his experiments with dogs. Think about what motivates you. What propels you to achieve your goals?

Many times over the years I have asked the students who have attended my seminars what motivates them. They consistently give four responses:

1. Money

2. Security

3. Self-respect

4. Recognition

I believe this list accurately represents those things that motivate all of us in life. The job search process can be difficult. It can be downright grueling at times. People tend not to be motivated in the face of rejection. However, daily recognition of what motivates you will keep your attitude healthy and in perspective. I suggest you write down your motivators on a small piece of paper. Place them in your wallet and review them when you need an extra punch to keep you going. Surely this is one good way to maintain a positive attitude. In the next chapter, we will discuss other ways.

Take a moment to fill out the next two pages of goal-setting exercises. You will discover much about yourself and begin to formulate exactly what it is that makes you happy and will also make you money.

After you complete the following exercises, you will discover some simple methods to help draw conclusions from your answers and help you create personal goal strategies.

IDENTIFICATION OF LIKES AND DISLIKES

List all the things you generally like and dislike. This is a brainstorming session, so there are no right or wrong answers. Also, keep in mind that no answer is too trite. All responses are valid.

LIKES	DISLIKES
Example: Working with and around people	Numbers, details, and desk work

IDENTIFICATION OF STRENGTHS AND WEAKNESSES

List what you believe to be your strengths and weaknesses. Again, this is a brainstorming session, so there are no right or wrong answers. Also, keep in mind that no answer it too trite. All responses are valid.

STRENGTHS	WEAKNESSES
Example: Good telephone voice Effective use of the telephone in a business setting	Financial reports and spreadsheets

FUNDAMENTAL GOAL-SETTING QUESTIONS AND ANSWERS

Answer the following questions openly and honestly. This is not a time to color the facts. In this exercise, as well, there are no right or wrong answers.

QUESTIONS	ANSWERS
1. What are your salary requirements?	
2. Under what circumstances would you be willing to take less? How much less?	
3. If you were offered a job that guaranteed you complete job and career happiness but paid much less, would you take it?	
4. Where do you want to be in your career one year from now?	
5. Where do you want to be in your career five years from now?	
6. What motivates you to be successful with your life and career?	
7. What personal obstacles are you aware of that may keep you from achieving your goals?	
8. Are you willing to take action and remove these obstacles?	
9. What actions are necessary in your opinion?	

First, let's take a look at your likes and dislikes. By focusing on your preferences, you can begin to determine the ideal job that would make you happy. As discussed earlier, the things that make you happy also make you money. Your dislikes reveal what you should consider ruling out as a major career focus. Unfortunately, some of your dislikes will come along with any career, no matter how compatible the job is with your likes.

Let's say, for instance, the first example under likes and dislikes on page 11 was written by you. You've stated that you like working with and around people. This realization is important. You should interview for jobs that will give you interaction with people. Rule out a cloistered position in a two-room office, preparing reports. It's not you. Sounds obvious, but often individuals take positions that they are dissatisfied with after only a few months. The reason they feel frustrated is that the job they have taken is fundamentally opposite to their basic likes.

Take a look at your strengths and weaknesses. Let's say the first example on page 12 was written by you. You have stated that you have a good phone voice and know how to use the telephone effectively in business. Begin to brainstorm by writing a list of jobs, such as airline reservations, telephone sales, and customer service positions, that would fit that description. Don't stop until you list at least ten careers for each strength.

After you have made your list, review the answers you wrote for the questions segment of this goal-setting exercise on page 13. Now, on a plain sheet of paper, write a master list of twenty-five job opportunities (be as specific as possible) that are congruent with the answers to these questions and that play on your likes and strengths. Do not stop writing until you have listed all twenty-five opportunities.

Ultimately, the purpose of goal-setting is to eliminate concerns and worries. Do you worry about your future? Replace worry with clear direction combined with action. Individuals who worry always can think of reasons why it is impossible to take action and improve their condition. Excuses simply prolong the pain and retard the ability to find a solution. Denis Waitley states in his book, *The Psychology of Winning*, "Losers do what is quick and easy" whereas winners "do what is difficult and necessary." I hope you have made a commitment to live by the formula of winners.

With this in mind and when you have completed the exercises in this chapter, you are now ready to begin the quest for the right career.

2

START WITH A POSITIVE ATTITUDE

Getting the job you want depends more on how you think rather than on something you do. According to Dr. Denis Waitley, author of *The Psychology of Winning*, a positive attitude is the single most important asset to achieving goals in life and being respected by others as a winner. Dr. Waitley states, "Before any Super Bowl team has won and long before an Olympic athlete takes the gold, each has visualized and believed that they are a winner."

The mind is the beginning of the reality you create for yourself. Each day you program your mind much like a computer programmer sets up a computer. There is a computer term that you may be familiar with—GIGO, or garbage in, garbage out. What are you programming your mind with?

1 **If you think you can't, you won't.**
If you think you can, you will!

We speak to ourselves and create our own programming at a rate of over 1,000 words per minute. This is what is meant by *self-talk*. Some things that happen to us, like the weather, are out of our control. But, for the most part, reality is a direct result of your beliefs and what you say to yourself. For instance, if someone believes consciously or unconsciously that he is never going to get promoted, or that she will never be good enough at computers to get a better job, then these individuals will act out those beliefs in their mind with negative internal chatter or *self-talk*. The resulting actions, or should I say, nonactions, make their negative beliefs come true.

2 **Practice positive self-talk:
"I can! I will! I know I can do it!"**

As you begin your thirty-day success plan, I have a very important question to ask you: What is your self-talk? What do you say to yourself when you lie in bed ready to fall asleep at night? What do you say to yourself when you awaken in the morning and contemplate a new day of activities? What are you thinking during your waking hours or daydreaming about over a cup of coffee? Be honest!

A winner's positive self-talk will sound something like this:

I know I can do it!

I have the drive, spirit and stamina to be successful!

I always achieve what I set my mind to do!

I'm the best, and I know others respect and like me as well!

I like myself!

I take full responsibility for myself and nothing can stop me from achieving my goals!

Bestselling author and behavioral researcher Dr. Shad Helmstetter has conducted extensive research in the area of self-talk. He states, "I have received thousands of letters from people who, in the middle of their adulthood, realized that they had believed something about themselves all their lives that was totally false. One man in particular," he remembers, "had never finished high school. His parents often said to others that their son ' . . . was not as smart as his sisters.' Another man, an alcoholic, had been told repeatedly while growing up that he, ' . . . was just like his father,' who also was an alcoholic." Here is a list of many untruths, the negative self-talk people entertain about themselves every day.

THE DESTRUCTIVE AFFIRMATIONS

The following is a sample list of the most frequently used phrases many of us say to ourselves, that in the end, sabotage our own quest for success. Place a check mark next to the phrases you have said to yourself either seriously or in jest.

I can't remember names.

It's going to be another one of those days.

It's just no use!

I just know it won't work.

Nothing ever goes right for me.

That's just my luck.

I'm so clumsy.

I don't have the talent.

I've never been good at that.

I'm just not creative.

Everything I eat goes right to my waist.

I've tried everything; nothing works!

I can't seem to get organized.

I don't care.

Today isn't my day!

I can never afford the things I want.

I already know I won't like it.

Why even try? I know already it won't work.

No matter what I do, I can't seem to lose the weight.

I never have enough time.

I just don't have the patience for that.

That really makes me mad!

It's another typical Monday.

When will I ever learn?

It won't work; face it.

I get sick just thinking about it.

Sometimes I just hate myself.

I'm just no good!

I'm too shy.

I never get any respect.

I never know what to say.

With my luck, I'll trip and fall.

With my luck, I don't have a chance.

I'd like to stop smoking, but I can't seem to quit.

Things just aren't working out for me right now.

I don't have the energy I used to.

I'm really out of shape.

I never have any money leftover at the end of the month.

Why should I try? It's not going to work anyway.

I'll never get promoted.

My desk is always a mess.

I can never find anything.

The only kind of luck I have is bad luck.

I never win anything.

I always lose.

I feel like I'm over the hill.

Someone always beats me to it.

Nobody likes me.

I'll never find a good job.

Source: Dr. Shad Helmstetter

Well, how did you do? Don't feel bad if you checked many of the phrases in the above exercise. However, if your self-talk sounds like the list above, it's never too late to join the team of winners in life. You can take action and break old habits of self-talk. Utilize this simple but life-changing principle that can make you a winner, too.

3 | **Neutralize negative self-talk ("I'll never find a good job.") with positive, winning statements.**

Change your negative programming with opposite, positive statements. Whether at home or driving in your car, speak to yourself out loud, or if others are around, in your mind. Make statements such as:

I like myself!

I know the interviewer will like me, too!

I am qualified for the job.

I am the best at what I do.

They will hire me.

There is no such thing as luck.

I always achieve what I set out to do.

Also, speak to yourself with simple, positive statements such as, "I can."

You can learn more about self-talk and the impact it has on your life by visiting Dr. Shad Helmstetter's site on the World Wide Web. Go to <http://www.monsoon.org>. Once you have arrived, scroll down to *The Self-talk Solution.* Click on its icon, and you're on your way to learning how to create more positive internal chatter resulting in a positive reality for your life and career.

I'd like to share a story to illustrate the role the power of the mind plays in each of our successes. Just like many of you reading this book, I was in the job market some years ago, right after graduation from college. With no job offer waiting for me, I decided to return home for the summer. Determined, I began sending out résumés to positions available all over the country. After two months, I was frustrated with little response to my efforts.

Then I met Leonard Evans, an older gentleman who was pastor of a large congregation in town. I knew of his reputation as a wise confidant. I also knew he was well connected with wealthy area businessmen. I called him for a lunch date, and he accepted.

At an Oriental restaurant, over moo goo gai pan, his favorite dish, he listened to a young man communicate the hopes, dreams, frustrations, and inability to find himself. I was doing all the talking. I figured if I sounded hard-luck enough, he would just call one of his business contacts and tell them to give me a job. That was not the case. What he did tell me when I finally shut up was more valuable than a job.

Somewhere between the main course and the fortune cookies, he queried, "Gary, have you ever read the story, 'Acres of Diamonds'?" "No," I replied, but I thought to myself, *The last thing I need is another book to read after five years of college.* He continued, "It is a true story written around the turn of the century. I suggest you read it, but I'll briefly tell you the story now.

"There was a man and his family who lived on a farm in the parched desert of the Mideast. The man's family had lived there for many generations. He was tired of the problems of irrigation and the poverty that came with being a tiller of the land.

"One day, he decided to take his family and search the world for more money and a better life. But first, he had to sell the farm, and that he did for a pittance. After years of travel throughout Europe, he was no better off and still searching.

"Then the news came that devastated his soul. A message arrived by wire that the family he sold his farm to had discovered acres of diamonds and found good fortune in their own backyard!''

Leonard looked at me with peaceful confidence and said, ''You've been working hard, looking everywhere to find a job and, more importantly, to find your purpose in life. What I am suggesting to you through this story is that your success is first in your own mind. Your mind is your own backyard. Believe in yourself, and you can bring about success, no matter where you live, no matter where you are, and under whatever circumstances life gives you.''

That was the most important lunch I will ever have. Not too many weeks later, I found a job in my own hometown, despite 12 percent unemployment. More importantly, I discovered a universal truth that keeps my life successful to this very day.

I hope you will go to the library and read 'Acres of Diamonds.' Realize its truth: Quit fighting. Stop struggling. Look inside yourself, analyze your strengths, identify your skills, and be positive about where you are in life. Your acres of diamonds are in your own backyard.

> **4** **Don't blame others. Take responsibility for yourself and your career. Don't blame previous jobs, bosses, or even your family for your current situation.**

Avoid blaming previous jobs, bosses, family, or even parents for your current situation. As long as you make excuses

25

for your problems in life, you will never take active, personal responsibility for yourself. You'll always rely on someone or something else to make you successful. That only happens to Cinderella! In real life, you have to make it happen.

Winners realize that adverse circumstances are a fact of life. Voltaire, the great French philosopher, likened life to being dealt a hand of cards. What you personally do with the cards determines your success.

Some individuals dwell on their negative past when they were a child or a teenager. Over and over they bitterly recount the same parental incidents that explain why they are so miserable today. I hope you avoid this pitfall. Admit the past, but don't let it control you. The past cannot be changed. Circumstances cannot be changed. You cannot control external situations. You can control your reaction to them and take clear, concise, and positive action. Essentially, anyone can make lemonade out of lemons.

5 **Practice visualization. When you lie awake in the morning or evening, visualize already working at and enjoying the career you want.**

Visualization is the key action step to creating and reinforcing a positive attitude. When you lie awake in the morning or evening, visualize already working at and enjoying the career you want.

Many people wonder what is meant by the term *visuali-*

zation. It is not necessary to see images. Some people simply state positive affirmations in their mind, similar to the self-talk of winners described earlier. Other people prefer to picture themselves occupied in successful activities. Whichever technique you choose, you must set aside a quiet time every day for visualization.

With visualization, you can take positive action to assure a positive attitude. See yourself working successfully at your ideal job or replay successful events from your past in your mind. Write ten personal positive affirmations you will use in your visualization time.

For example, write down:

Each day I get better and better.

I have everything I need inside of me to become successful.

I am a dynamic and well-liked person.

I feel healthy.

I am happy.

I know I can do it.

You can literally create hundreds more affirmations and visualizations.

TEN PERSONAL POSITIVE AFFIRMATIONS

1.	
2.	
3.	
4.	
5.	
6.	
7.	
8.	
9.	
10.	

Every day you should use the ten affirmations you just completed. Add to them often, and get quality quiet time to visualize them.

> **6** Dress like a winner. Make sure your clothes are clean and pressed. Make sure your hair and image are clean and simple.

A successful person in life not only thinks like a winner but also dresses like a winner. Make sure your clothes are clean and pressed and your hair and image are clean and simple.

According to research, verbal content comprises only 7 percent of your total message. Your visual image comprises 93 percent of the message you convey to others. What you say is only a small part of what others perceive you to be.

According to Janet Elsea's book, *The Four Minute Sell,* an interview is decided within the first four minutes based on image. Others would argue that it is actually thirty seconds or less.

A negative first impression may make it difficult or impossible to sell, influence, or persuade someone. Think of a recent time when you attended a party or family gathering and you met new people. Did they make a positive or negative first impression on you? If it was positive, how so? If it was negative, what turned you off? Was it their mannerisms, hair, clothes, jewelry, perfume, or aftershave? Remember, you never get a second chance to make a good first impression.

I remember the time I had to interview a number of individuals for the position of an on-site computer trainer. All day long, the applicants drifted in for their appointments. The secretary had each wait in the reception area. Nothing out of the ordinary happened until a young lady arrived dressed in Easter Sunday church attire: large yellow rim hat, yellow shoes, and a yellow-and-orange dress. The outfit was beautiful, but it stuck out like a sore thumb in a business environment. It stuck out so much that the other employees were still talking about the job seeker a year later. The other six individuals that interviewed were long forgotten. In business, you want to draw attention to your skills, not your looks. When you leave an interview, you want the interviewer to remember you, not something you were wearing.

You can control your image to suit the company intending to interview you. If you believe it is in your best interests to look older, then dress more conservatively. Wear quality accessories. Should you feel it is in your best interests to look younger, wear shorter hair and a slightly more updated wardrobe. Your image can influence others in any direction you wish to take them.

Wear the appropriate image for the company and industry you would like to enter. Are you sabotaging yourself by *not* dressing the part? When necessary, wear the conservative suit of Wall Street or the casual wear of the Silicon Valley. Individuals who have successful interviews are those who have also mastered the correct image for the situation. Avoid getting locked into one look for all interviews. Put some thought into the company and position, then dress accordingly. Whatever the case may be, the fact remains: Image sells!

Research shows that the two most important visual cues interviewers look at are an interviewee's hair and shoes. They start at the top and go directly to the bottom. "Which means, in theory, you could arrive naked as long as you have well-combed hair and shiny shoes. However, this is only a theory, and is not recommended,'' jokingly states Camille Lavington, a career specialist at a division of the Sara Lee Corporation.

THE COMPONENTS OF IMAGE

Just for the record, when we discuss image and its impact on an interviewer in the first thirty seconds, here are its main components:

Hair

Shoes

Clothing

Hands

Fingernails

Skin

Hygiene

Perfume or cologne

Makeup

Jewelry

Teeth

Facial expressions

Body language

Accessories

Voice tone/pitch/quality

Manners/politeness/etiquette

Take action on your image. Stop a moment and take inventory of your professional wardrobe and accessories with the following exercise. If you check off items that need to be replaced, consider borrowing those items from a friend or family member. You will save money and accomplish the same result.

PROFESSIONAL ATTIRE INVENTORY

ITEM	HAVE	DON'T HAVE	NEEDS REPLACING
1. Interview suit			
2. Alternate suit			
3. Shirt/blouse			
4. Polished shoes			
5. Tie (men)			
6. Black notebook			
7. Attractive watch			
8. Professional pen			
9. Other accessories: _____ _____ _____			

A common misconception about image is the notion that you need to make a statement of individuality when appearing in public. Save the trendy jewelry, shaved head, and strangely pierced body parts for parties and weekends. If you want career success, then dress the part at all business-related activities. This includes even after-hours business-related parties and dinners. Trendy dressing is better for your career when kept for parties among family and friends.

Let's review now what we've learned in this first chapter:

1. If you think you can't, you won't.

2. Practice positive self-talk.

3. Neutralize negative self-talk with positive statements.

4. Take responsibility for your own life.

5. Practice visualization.

6. Dress like a winner.

3

PREPARE A SUCCESSFUL
RÉSUMÉ AND COVER LETTER

A common misconception most job seekers have is that recruiters and managers have plenty of time to read résumés. For more than five years, I have been personally acquainted with many of the recruitment directors for the nation's leading companies. They would agree that their job is much more complex than reading résumés and hiring employees. Like all business professionals, they have meetings, travel, and perform other tasks related to their job. Essentially, they are very busy people.

> **7** Design a one-page résumé. Give just enough information to prompt an interview. Leave the reader wanting more.

For this reason, when dealing with recruiters, maintain the KISS principle. My version is: Keep It Simple, Salesperson! You're selling yourself. As it is with most things in life, the most convincing and the most profound concepts are those that are stated in the simplest terms. The fast-paced business world of recruiters, overwhelmed by travel, fax machines, deadlines, and computers, demands a one-page résumé, which can be reviewed quickly. When you create an informative, one-page résumé, you have achieved two important factors in your favor: First, your one-page résumé saves the recruiter valuable time and is more likely to be read. Second, you have given the recruiter just enough information to prompt an interview and find out more. You'll be getting more phone calls than your competition.

Often, job seekers attending my seminars discuss with me their objections to a one-page résumé. The most common one I hear is, "Yes, but you just don't seem to understand. I've had all these years of experience, and in so many words, I'm so great and wonderful, it can't possibly be told on one page!" My response to this objection is, in the words of Brian Tracy, author of *The Psychology of Success*, "Well, go try it twenty times, if it still doesn't work, call and tell me, then go back and do it your way."

Stick to the formula. It works! Don't try to tell your whole story on paper. Leave the reader wanting more. Don't feel obligated to list every day of every year since you began working. If you have been working for a few years, omit months in your chronology of dates. Just list the years. It's easier to read. Only include the experience relevant to the job for which you are applying. If you just graduated, list your education near the beginning of the résumé. If you have been employed for a few years, list your education near the end. Your work history, what you have accomplished, is more important.

In the high-tech age of personal computers, desktop publishing, computerized spell checks, and laser printers, there is no excuse for a scruffy-looking résumé. Your competition is making use of technology and so should you. A program like WordPerfect for Windows or Microsoft Word should be used to produce your résumé. In WordPerfect, for example, the user is provided with three résumé template options: Contemporary, Cosmopolitan, and Traditional. To reach this option, click on File, then New, and scroll down in Group to Resume. Complete the template with your particular data. It's that simple. Next, print it out with a laser printer. The result is a spectacular-looking and professional résumé.

> 8 **Print out your résumé on white paper only, using a professional résumé computer software template. Use spell check and make sure that your grammar is correct.**

Unless you are looking for a position in advertising, art, or design, stay clear of colorful and trendy-looking résumés. Often, people choose colorful paper for their résumés because they think that color increases recognition by the recruiter. However, you run the risk that a recruiter will not like that color and will think the résumé looks trendy and denotes instability. It's better to have your résumé look too conservative than to risk it looking too flashy. The bottom line is that white is always appropriate. However, one way to achieve increased recognition in a large stack of résumés is to select a high-quality linen stock paper. Go to your local print shop and browse through what will surely be an excellent selection of fine linen papers.

There are other pitfalls, traps that résumé writers fall into unknowingly. Beware! Here are my top ten résumé writing pitfalls to avoid.

THE TOP TEN RÉSUMÉ WRITING PITFALLS TO AVOID

1. Too long

2. Scattered: The information does not flow; hard to follow

3. Big sentences, big paragraphs, too much that says too little

4. Small type (never go smaller than twelve points) and bad printer

5. Sparse: looks like you never did anything at your last job(s)

6. Few white spaces

7. Listing of height, weight, marital status, sex, health (Who cares?)

8. Spell check that did not catch everything, i.e. *there's* instead of *theirs,* other typographical errors, and poor grammar

9. Too many typefaces, too fancy, too busy, resulting in too distracting

10. Lacks a target: It arrives on someone's desk with no clear application for their need; lacking target language

Now that you are convinced that a one-page résumé is in your best interests, I've got good news for you: There is a time and a place for an expanded two- or three-page résumé. Briefly, here's how it works. The one-page résumé is utilized for cold leads. For instance, a newspaper ad would be considered a cold lead. Send a one-page résumé to companies with which you have no personal contact, or where no personal referral from a friend has helped get your foot in the door.

The expanded two- or three-page résumé is utilized for warm leads. For instance, a referral by a family member asking you to contact a hiring manager friend would be considered a warm lead. Send the two- or three-page résumé to individuals and companies that you are personally referred to, who you know will give you personalized attention. Also, the expanded résumé makes a great leave-behind at the close of the first interview that you got as a result of sending in your one-page résumé.

Following is Gregory Miller's two-page résumé, which is to be used for warm leads. Directly following it is the edited one-page résumé version, to be used for cold leads. Miller's résumé is an excellent format for anyone who is not a recent graduate and has been in a career for some time. Stephanie Chambers's résumé follows next. Her young career and limited work history make the résumé naturally one page. It is an excellent format for anyone who is just graduating and is beginning to embark on a career. Adapt these formats to your own information.

Gregory E. Miller
184 Main Street
State College, PA 16804
(814) 237-3012
a.v.guru@guno.com

SUMMARY OF QUALIFICATIONS

• Over ten years of experience in audiovisual management production
• Extensive experience in electronics training programs design and facilitation
• Comprehensive knowledge of computers, software, and networks
• Extensive experience in new facility electronic systems design and implementation
• Excellent written and oral communication skills

WORK EXPERIENCE

• 1993–Present   The Scanticon Conference
  Position: Manager Audiovisual   Center Hotel
                                           State College, Pennsylvania

Managed audiovisual technology for a 26,750-square-foot, state-of-the-art conference center. Oversaw final stages of the facility's construction and equipment installation. Recruited, trained, and managed a staff of twelve. Upgraded the center's technical equipment needs based on changing requirements from its original investment of $1.3 million. Responsible for the maintenance and repair of all equipment. Exceeded top management's expectations of my position.

• 1992–1993   The State College School District
  Position: Instructor   State College, Pennsylvania

Responsible for the instruction of over 100 high-school-level electronics students. Designed custom curriculums and selected appropriate textbooks. Personally developed laboratory experiments, specified and ordered $10,000 in lab materials, and conducted all classes.

• 1991-1992   National Baseball Hall of Fame
  Position: Independent Contractor   Cooperstown, New York

Conducted a needs assessment of the client's multimedia theater. Designed and prototyped all circuitry, conducted tests, designed circuit boards, and installed a $2 million theater system. Wrote and produced documentation for the system.

• 1990–1991   The Pennsylvania State University
  Position: Independent Contractor   State College, Pennsylvania

Developed theatrical electrical systems for the Carnegie Building Cinema. Specified acoustics, seating, layout, and the relevant architectural features of the facility. Coordinated efforts with the university's physical plant, architect, vendors, and subcontractors. Conducted an initial on-site needs assessment. Generated written specifications and detailed construction drawings. Installed projection, audio, and theatrical lighting systems.

• **1986–1990**	**Pennsylvania Network, Inc.**
Position: Independent Contractor	**Philadelphia, Pennsylvania**

Designed, specified, installed, and repaired all electronic systems, including telephone PBX and satellite reception technology for this news network. Developed and constructed a PC-based digital control system for the automated operation of all network audio feeds. Communicated with broadcast engineers At sixty affiliate stations regarding downlink operations and other technical matters.

EDUCATION
• B.A. Broadcasting, The Pennsylvania State University, State College, Pennsylvania
• FCC General Radiotelephone and First Class Radiotelephone Licenses
• Certificate, Dale Carnegie Institute, The Penn State Scanticon Conference Center

AWARDS AND ACHIEVEMENTS
• Member, Society of Broadcast Engineers
• Member, Society of Motion Picture and Television Engineers
• Pennsylvania Network, Loyal Service and Dedication Award
• Who's Who among Colleges and Universities

REFERENCES
• Available upon request

Before we take a look at Gregory Miller's one-page résumé, take a moment to recognize why his two-page format is reader friendly.

RÉSUMÉ READABILITY ENHANCEMENTS

Enhance your résumé's readability by using the following:

- *Bold.* Notice how it draws your eyes to key sections.

- *Bullets.* Surveys have shown that almost 75 percent of recruiters prefer reading a résumé with bullets.

- *Indentations.* Creates lots of white, open spaces.

- *Large headlines.* Also draws your eyes to key sections.

- *Summary of qualifications.* Lists a few hot selling features about you. Makes the reader want to learn more. Also use this area to address every requirement in an advertisement. Same principle as headlines in a newspaper.

- *Awards and achievements.* Everyone has them. Take some time and come up with a few. Without this section you appear *average.*

Okay, now that you know why Miller's résumé is effective, notice how in the next section it has been ruthlessly (but necessarily) edited to just key points resulting in a one-page document. Take note of how the bold, bullets, indentations, large headlines, etc., have remained intact. After reading this section, begin to work on your own two- and one-page résumé in a computer program like WordPerfect following Gregory Miller's résumé as your official format. It works, so don't change it!

Gregory E. Miller
184 Main Street
State College, PA 16804
(814) 237-3012
a.v.guru@guno.com

SUMMARY OF QUALIFICATIONS

- Over ten years of experience in audiovisual management production
- Extensive experience in electronics training programs design and facilitation
- Comprehensive knowledge of computers, software, and networks
- Extensive experience in new facility electronic systems design and implementation

WORK EXPERIENCE

- **1993–Present**   **The Scanticon Conference**
  Position: Manager Audiovisual   **Center Hotel**
                                                      State College, Pennsylvania

Managed audiovisual technology for a 26,750-square-foot state-of-the-art conference center. Recruited, trained, and managed a staff of twelve. Exceeded management's expectations.

- **1992–1993**   **The State College School District**
  Position: Instructor   **State College, Pennsylvania**

Responsible for the instruction of over 100 high-school-level electronics students. Designed custom curriculums and selected appropriate textbooks.

- **1990–1992**   **National Baseball Hall of Fame**
  Position: Independent Contractor   **Cooperstown, New York**

Designed all circuitry, circuit boards, and installed the client's theater system. During this time period, also developed theatrical electrical systems for the Carnegie Building Cinema at The Pennsylvania State University, State College, Pennsylvania.

- **1986–1990**   **Pennsylvania Network, Inc.**
  Position: Manager Electronic Systems   **Philadelphia, Pennsylvania**

Designed, specified, installed, and repaired all electronic systems, including telephone PBX and satellite reception technology for this news network.

EDUCATION

- B.A. Broadcasting, The Pennsylvania State University, State College, Pennsylvania

AWARDS AND ACHIEVEMENTS

- Member, Society of Broadcast Engineers
- Member, Society of Motion Picture and Television Engineers
- Pennsylvania Network, Loyal Service and Dedication Award

REFERENCES

- Available upon request

Stephanie K. Chambers
10 River Street
Bellefonte, PA 16339
(814) 788-8840
stephaniek@aol.com

SUMMARY OF QUALIFICATIONS
- Successful completion of B.S. in Business Administration and Marketing
- Over three years of work-study experience at all administration finance levels
- Excellent computer skills: Excel, Lotus, Microsoft, Windows, and WordPerfect
- Monthly output of $600,000 in invoices
- Detailed and accurate organizational skills

EDUCATION
- B.S. Business Administration and Marketing, Mansfield University, Mansfield, Pennsylvania

WORK EXPERIENCE
- **1995–Present**   **The Scanticon Conference**
  Position: Accounts Payable   **Center Hotel**
                                   State College, Pennsylvania

Responsible for processing all invoices and authorizing check payments in accordance with the Conference Center's activity of $600,000 per month. Reconcile daily statements and month-end balancing of payables. Maintain spreadsheets in Excel. Responsible for monthly accruals of $16,000.

- **1994–1995**   **Keystone Community Services**
  Position: Bookkeeper/Receptionist   **Bellefonte, Pennsylvania**

Handled the preparation of monthly invoices, check payments, answering phone calls, and greeting clients. Reconciled monthly bank statements. Maintained client files and kept information confidential. Prepared budgets in excess of $70,000.

AWARDS AND ACHIEVEMENTS
- Who's Who Among Colleges and Universities
- Phi Beta Lambda, Business Fraternity, Parliamentarian

REFERENCES
- Available upon request

Now that your two-page résumé is edited down to one page and on white paper, what gives your résumés the punch you need to get the reader to act? Action words!

9

Utilize action words constantly throughout the résumé. Take the time to be creative; use a thesaurus to avoid duplication of action words.

Make every word in your résumé count. This is the same strategy that print advertisers use. Each word must say something important to the reader. After all, you, like an advertiser, want the reader to take action. An advertiser wants you to buy a product. You want a recruiter to pick up the phone and call you.

Look back at the résumés on the previous pages. Underline the action words. Next, read the following list of action words specially prepared to help get you started. Use them and extract a list of ten words that will uniquely apply to you when preparing or revising your résumé.

When creating a résumé or a cover letter, use action words to summarize what actions were taken and what results occurred. Always provide numbers, dollars, percentages, and increases. Numbers quantify your value or worth to a prospective employer. They show responsibility. For instance, saying you "recruited, trained, and managed the tech support staff" is a weak statement. A stronger statement is, you "recruited, trained, and managed a tech support staff of twelve." To become better familiar with how to integrate numbers into your own résumé, look back at the résumés on the previous pages and underline the instances where numbers were used.

ACTION WORDS

accomplished	enforced	modified	revived
achieved	engineered	monitored	saved
acquired	established	motivated	scheduled
adapted	evaluated	negotiated	selected
administered	examined	obtained	served
advanced	exceeded	operated	set up
analyzed	executed	ordered	settled
applied	expanded	organized	shaped
arranged	expedited	originated	showed
assessed	financed	overcame	simplified
assigned	forecasted	oversaw	sold
assisted	formed	participated	solved
attained	formulated	performed	specified
audited	found	pioneered	sponsored
bought	founded	planned	staffed
broadened	fulfilled	prepared	standardized
brought	generated	presented	started
calculated	guided	prevented	stimulated
centralized	handled	processed	streamlined
collaborated	headed	produced	strengthened
completed	hired	programmed	studied
composed	identified	projected	suggested
conceived	implemented	promoted	summarized
concluded	improved	proved	supervised
conducted	improvised	provided	supported
consolidated	increased	published	surpassed
constructed	influenced	purchased	surveyed
consulted	initiated	realized	taught
contributed	instituted	recommended	terminated
controlled	instructed	reconciled	tested
coordinated	insured	recruited	tightened
created	integrated	redesigned	traded
cut	interpreted	reduced	trained
decreased	interviewed	regulated	transacted
delivered	introduced	reinforced	transferred
demonstrated	invented	rejected	transformed
designed	invested	related	translated
determined	investigated	renegotiated	trimmed
developed	led	reorganized	tripled
devised	liquidated	reported	undertook
directed	located	represented	unified
distributed	made	researched	used
documented	maintained	reshaped	utilized
doubled	managed	resolved	verified
earned	marketed	restored	vitalized
edited	mediated	reviewed	withdrew
eliminated	minimized	revised	worked

PERSONAL ACTION WORDS

Write ten sentences utilizing ten action words that best describe your work history.

1.
2.
3.
4.
5.
6.
7.
8.
9.
10.

There is one final factor that determines a successful résumé.

10

Target the résumé to each particular company and position.

Targeting your résumé should conjure up images of hitting the bull's-eye on a dartboard or shooting arrows at a practice target. That kind of accuracy is exactly what is required every time you send out a résumé. A common mistake is to produce one résumé and send it out generically to all companies. I'd like to give you an example of what I mean by targeting your résumé. Consider a person applying for a management job at a manufacturing facility. The résumé obviously will communicate the previous job skills that demonstrate effective management of both employees and operations. Conversely, this same individual, when applying for a customer service management position, must also interject action words that demonstrate a successful track record servicing and maintaining customer satisfaction.

The first résumé should not be sent to apply for the second position. It would not contain the customer service target language that would be likely to get a callback and interview.

Now we'll do one together. Say an individual is applying for the position of receptionist at a law firm. The position requires PBX operations and greeting clients. What skills would the résumé emphasize? Mainly, the applicant would emphasize previous PBX experience and the ability, when under pressure, to interact with others and be pleasant.

If this same person applied for a job as a receptionist to a CPA who required light bookkeeping, what additional skills would be interjected into the new résumé? The applicant would need to demonstrate successful implementation of organizational and analytical skills. If at all possible, the résumé should be slanted from a bookkeeping perspective.

In order to target your résumé quickly on a daily basis, you need consistent access to a computer and laser printer. Maintain a computer disk of your résumés and cover letters so that you can transport the documents and edit them on a home, office, or school computer. Store multiple résumés for various applications. If you don't have easy access to a computer, contact a twenty-four-hour business center like Kinko's. They will help you edit your résumé and cover letters for a minimum charge. For computer literate individuals, they will supply you with a computer workstation. You can do it yourself and save money. Write each résumé to target positions that you are applying to throughout your job search and that are congruent with your previous work history.

THE ELECTRONIC RÉSUMÉ

Posting a résumé on-line is a different art all its own. Web sites like *Résumés On-Line* provide employers the ability to search for prospective employees. Human resources directors and hiring managers find a wide variety of quality personnel by retrieving your résumé, arranged by category and posted on-line. The cost? A one page résumé online can range from free to a few dollars a month. To inquire about placing your résumé on-line with *Résumés On-Line*, inquire at <hhog@hog.com>.

Writing a résumé on-line can be done in various ways. Some on-line services provide you with a screen form to fill out, which in turn generates an electronic résumé for their database. Other companies require that you send a copy of your original résumé on disk or download it via modem. One company, *CareerMosaic*, not only gives you the ability to post your résumé but also to communicate with and research prospective employers. Using a search engine like *Infoseek* or *Yahoo*, type *CareerMosaic* at the search prompt to enter the realm of virtual résumés and job searching.

According to *CareerMosaic*, ''Real people find real jobs on line.'' One newly employed graduate wrote, ''I responded to an ad under your JOBS database and I started my job within two weeks.'' Another person states, *''CareerMosaic* was invaluable in finding me my new job. [After posting the résumé] recruiters were calling me daily.'' Personally, I know firsthand the success of posting a résumé on-line. I just recently assisted in the recruitment of a manager for a major hotel company after discovering his résumé on-line.

ELECTRONIC RÉSUMÉ WRITING TIPS

• *Use nouns.* Forget what I said in the previous section about action words and descriptives. The name of the game here is nouns. Computers search for key words such as biotech, engineer, programmer, and administrator.

• *Use keywords.* Think about the top ten keywords that someone, if they were looking for you, would use to find you if they typed in a word search string. Integrate all of those words into your résumé. For instance, if you are a food and beverage manager, your keywords may be: restaurant, bar, food service, hotel, banquets, dining, menu, cuisine, food manager and beverage manager.

• *KISS (Keep It Simple, Salesperson!).* We've learned this before, but the same holds true for electronic résumés. Avoid decorative typefaces and too much underlining. In cyberspace, just the facts!

• *Name and contact first.* You're selling yourself, so keep your contact information prominent in the résumé.

• *Avoid jargon.* Minimize the use of abbreviations and acronyms. Write using simple words that everyone knows and would be commonly used for your industry.

• *White spaces.* Same as the résumés we created earlier, computer screens like lots of white spaces.

52

- *One-page resume.* Keep it to one page for recent college graduates. One-, two-, and three-page résumés for executives and workers with extensive years in their careers and experience.

- *Minimize E-mail.* Do follow up, but avoid excessive E-mails to your on-line recruiters.

A final word of caution about electronic résumés: If you are currently employed, consider the fact that registering your résumé with an on-line résumé service exposes you to the risk that your current employer will read your posting. Remember, the more broadly you distribute your résumé, the more likely it will come back to your boss. One way to combat this if it is a valid concern of yours is to only list your résumé with an on-line database that promises anonymity. In this case, your résumé is accepted for distribution without your name and address. Companies will be able to reply to you via some type of E-mail address or registration number.

An effective cover letter is very calculated and follows key guidelines in much the same manner as a résumé.

11

> **A cover letter has three distinct paragraphs:**
>
> 1. ATTENTION. **The first paragraph gets the reader's attention with important facts or features about you.**
>
> 2. BENEFIT. **The second paragraph tells the company the benefits of hiring you.**
>
> 3. CLOSE FOR ACTION. **The last paragraph must close for the interview. Simply state, "When can an interview be arranged? I can be reached at [give your telephone number]."**

The first paragraph gets the reader's attention. This is where you interject a few outstanding facts or features about yourself. I remember a gentleman applying this advice after one of my college seminars a few years ago. He had cleaned pools in South Florida all through school. He felt there was nothing about cleaning pools that would get anyone's attention in his cover letter. He was about to prove me wrong, or so he thought. We began to discuss what he perceived to be a no-way-out situation. I asked how many pools he serviced when he first started. "Thirty-five," he replied. But then he remembered how, over the years, he acquired more customers because many of the pool owners referred him to their friends. Eventually, he had over fifty customers. Now, all of a sudden, he realized that he did have something significant to say about his achievements as a pool cleaner. He no longer was an inexperienced recent college graduate. He began to realize the special skills it took to maintain customers, acquire new ones, and be a loyal employee for many years. He put that in his cover letter, and he was offered a position at a major telecommunications company making $26,000 the first year. That's a world away from his self-proclaimed limitation of being just a pool cleaner.

Following is a sample cover letter that adheres to the guidelines I just discussed. It also contains portions of this individual's success story and how his cover letter would have looked.

The second paragraph of a cover letter tells the manager or recruiter the benefits of hiring you. This is where you don't just give them facts, you must give them corresponding benefits as well. For example, it is not enough to say you have received extensive training (that is a fact). Give them a benefit, too. In so many words, let them know that because you are trained, they will save valuable time and be able to give top priority to other department projects. If you can communicate this, you're very close to getting the job.

Never state a fact, feature, or advantage without stating a benefit to the other person. Without a corresponding benefit, the person you're speaking with has no clue as to how it will profit them. It can be further stated that facts, features, and advantages mean nothing without benefits. If you master the technique of fact plus benefit equals results, you will have an explosive tool for interviews. The only problem you'll have is deciding which job offer to take.

Because this technique is extremely valuable, be absolutely sure you are clear on how to construct, write, and state a fact plus a corresponding benefit. Fill out the worksheet on page 58. The first couple are done for you.

Joe Adams
3725 South Ocean Dr.
Hollywood Beach, FL 33020

January 12, 1997

Ms. Jane Melville
ABC Company
100 Company Boulevard
Miami, FL 33138

Dear Ms. Melville:

My résumé, which I have enclosed, presents my training and experience in sales and customer service over the past two years. I have successfully managed thirty-five customer accounts and effectively increased my customers to over fifty with Blue Water Pool Cleaning Service, where I currently work. This experience has given me a solid background in sales and customer service and will enable me to get results for your company.

I am known for my creativity, adaptability, initiative, and self-starter abilities. I am resourceful and can establish immediate rapport and long-lasting relationships with clients and colleagues. I can fit into your team plan quickly and effectively with minimal learning time to achieve immediate results.

Since you are in need of a strong sales associate, I have the ability to not only meet but exceed ABC Company's expectations. I believe I can explain in just a few minutes why I am a likely candidate for a position in sales and customer service with your company. When can we arrange an interview? I may be reached at (954) 555-4493.

Sincerely,

Joe Adams

Joe Adams
Enclosure

FACT-TO-BENEFIT WORKSHEET

Fact, Feature, or Advantage	Corresponding Benefit
1. I'm just out of college.	1. You will have an eager, energetic employee who will grow with and be dedicated to the company.
2. I have ten years' experience.	2. There will be minimum time wasted in training. Productivity will begin immediately.
3. I minored in that in college.	
4. Computers are my specialty.	
5. My previous boss liked how organized and professional I was.	
6. I haven't missed a day of work in two years.	
7. I always worked overtime whenever my boss asked.	
8. In my spare time, I volunteer at the American Red Cross giving workshops on AIDS awareness to teenagers.	
9. My parents taught me responsibility at an early age.	
10. My hobbies include sports and computers.	

In my opinion, the third paragraph of a cover letter is the shortest and easiest to construct, but many people seem to have a hard time doing it. Close for action, just like all the advertising mail you get for all those incredible one-time offers. Ask the reader to take action—to pick up the phone and call you. Ask, "When can we arrange an interview? I can be reached at [give them your telephone number]."

Do not rely on weak phrases such as, "Hope to hear from you soon," or phrases that set you up for failure, such as, "Thank you for your consideration. I'll be calling you." If they know you are going to call, they are going to make sure you don't get through. It is always better to get them to call you. When they call you, it is an indication that you are being pursued. This places you in a much better position to negotiate and sell yourself at the interview. If you must call them, don't announce it in your letter. Just plan on calling them about three to five business days after sending your information by conventional mail. If you faxed it, call within two to three days if you have not heard from the company.

Now that you have read this chapter, please *do not* try to get a job with your résumé and cover letter!

12

The purpose of the résumé and cover letter is to get you the interview.

Even the best résumé and cover letter are not likely to result in a job offer.

Most companies do not hire sight unseen. The interview is where you sell yourself and get the job.

A résumé and cover letter are just selling tools to get you an interview. The interview is where you will sell yourself and get the job offer.

Let's review what we have learned in this third chapter:

7. Design a one-page résumé.

8. Produce a professional résumé on white paper.

9. Utilize action words.

10. Target your résumé.

11. Create a cover letter with three distinct paragraphs. First, get their attention. Second, state benefits after facts, features, and advantages. Third, close for action. Ask when an interview may be arranged. Give them your phone number and ask them to call you.

12. Don't try to get a job with a résumé and cover letter. Their only purpose is to get you an interview.

4

DEVELOPING LEADS AND NETWORKING

Generating new leads and contacts is the single, most crucial activity you must perform daily to get the job you want. Spend your waking hours developing leads, amassing contacts, and networking. Getting the job you want is mostly a numbers game.

Gambling casinos work on the same system. Last year, I visited Monte Carlo and spent an evening for my first time ever at a casino. Knowing I was inexperienced, I immediately determined that dropping coins into a slot machine was my best bet. After cashing $50 into French ten-franc pieces, I cautiously began to drop one coin in at a time. I learned quickly. Every time I hit with one coin, I only received a measly two or three coins back. After taking notice of the odds and combination chart posted on the machine, I realized that in order to win a larger payback, I had to risk more coins. Winning two and three coins was not good enough for me. I was determined to win big and began placing two- and three-coin bets. After ten or more bets, nothing. I was concerned. Then it happened—a three-coin hit! The payback was at least fifty coins or better. I was hooked. Discovering my numbers game worked, I continued to play until 3:00 in the morning, winning a total of over $500!

Tom Jackson, author of *Guerrilla Tactics in the Job Market*, agrees that the job search is mostly a numbers game. He states, "Every job campaign looks much like this: NO, NO, NO, NO, NO, NO, NO, NO, NO, NO, NO, YES!"

Just like the casino illustration, every job campaign will be a long series of losses followed by a win. At least in the job market, you have better odds. You only have to get one yes. So please don't take the casino illustration out of context. I'll admit, I was lucky that night. However, the fact remains: If you don't play the numbers game, you can't win.

I am aware that many individuals have a deep-rooted fear of rejection. Although these people would agree in principle that getting a job is mostly a numbers game, they will never achieve their goals because a turndown is taken as a personal rejection. When a turndown is viewed negatively, the job search process actually goes into reverse. An individual will produce less contacts in order to be shielded from further disappointments. This is counterproductive to achieving the desired goal.

A turndown is actually a positive experience in much the same way as the casino illustration. Every loss I had put me one bet closer to a fifty-coin win. For every no you get, you are one step closer to that one yes. Just like losses at a slot machine, receiving rejections in a job campaign is part of the territory.

Brian Tracy, in his tape series *The Science of Self-Confidence*, states that "if you are not failing, you're not trying." Don't be afraid to fail. Reassess your attitude toward failure. Unfortunately, as children we often learn the wrong message about failure. We are punished for failure in many ways and quickly learn failure is to be avoided. As adults, we should have discovered the opposite, that success is always preceded by failure.

Thomas Edison, in his quest to make a lightbulb, performed thousands of experiments. Somewhere near experiment 10,000, he created the first lightbulb. Someone asked him how he felt about his failures. He responded, "I learned 10,000 ways how not to make a lightbulb." Through his thousands of experiments, Mr. Edison also discovered success is a numbers game. Try something long enough, in a number of different ways, with intelligent guesses along the way, and you will eventually succeed. History is marked with great failures who became great successes. The books are full of people who have failed often enough that they learned how to succeed.

You can tell how high or low a person is going to get in life by how they respond to rejection and failure. Losers see failure as indicative of their lack of talent and abilities. They become disappointed easily. Eventually, they become preoccupied with taking no further risks in life. They shield themselves from further disappointments. Brian Tracy states, "People that fear failure put their lives into reverse. They try fewer and fewer things and success avoids them." Winners, on the other hand, welcome failure. They realize that triumph over failure brings one over the edge to success.

How do you view the glass? Is it half empty or half full? Do you view a turndown as one step closer to defeat or one step closer to winning? Make a commitment today to increase the number of no's you are going to get. You now are on the fast track to getting the job you want.

Although you may agree with what I am saying in principle, you may still not have resolved a common but important question: "How do I remain motivated, even in a slump?"

In order to keep from getting into a slump and to get out of one, should you arrive there unaware, you must reward yourself when you meet daily goals. Realize that today's objective, in essence, is not to get a job. Today's objective is to perform the correct, consistent job-seeking activities you are learning in this book. Meeting your daily goals is your only concern. Getting the job you want will be an automatic result.

Becoming depressed and falling into a slump is a result of focusing on a job offer. Your mind can play tricks on you. It says you will only be happy when you get a job offer. The truth really is, your mind needs reprogramming. True happiness and well-being are achieved by accomplishing each day's objectives. An individual who meets daily goals has confidence that a job offer will result. This is the law of cause and effect, which means that what you get back is a direct result of what you put out. Meet your daily job-seeking goals, and you will get a job.

13

Secure six new leads a day (thirty a week) and send them your cover letter and résumé. (Boxes 14, 15, and 16 explain where to find new leads.)

This success formula requires selecting 30 new leads a week that are compatible with your particular career goals. That is only 6 new leads per day, working five days a week. The total comes out to 120 leads for the month. Accelerate your fast track to success even more and generate 6 new leads a day, working seven days a week. That total comes out to 180 leads for the month! It can be done, and your success is virtually guaranteed.

14 | **Secure ten leads a week from the newspaper's help-wanted section. Send your cover letter and résumé.**

The newspaper's help-wanted section must comprise only one-third of your total new leads. According to the U.S. Department of Labor, 85 percent of all jobs available are never published. If you rely on the newspaper for all of your leads, you're missing out on 85 percent of the jobs actually available. Worse yet, if 100 percent of the people are only reading the newspaper and vying for 15 percent of the jobs, where does that leave you?

15

> **Secure ten leads a week from cold calls. Simply drop in on ten businesses, leave a résumé, and get the name of the person who hires for your position. Go back home and mail them a cover letter and résumé. Better yet, try to see them while you are there.**

Cold-calling is a method that, when utilized, will get you creatively networking and connect you with the other 85 percent of the jobs that are unpublished. The term comes from what salespeople do when marketing certain types of products door-to-door. My version of cold-calling for job seekers means to simply drop in on ten businesses you would like to work for and leave your résumé with a secretary, supervisor, or manager.

While you are there, request the name or business card of the person who hires for your position. Return home and mail each contact your cover letter and résumé. Better yet, try to see the key person who hires for your position while you are there. The law of averages dictates that you will get an on-the-spot interview every few cold calls. These interviews could have taken weeks to arrange if you had relied on more traditional methods. You are weeks ahead of your competition.

After hearing this, I know already what you are thinking: *He must be crazy! There's no way I'm going to walk into a strange office and hand out my résumé! I'll just stick to the newspapers and mail résumés from home.*

To counter this objection, remember that the U.S. Department of Labor states that 85 percent of all jobs available are never published.

In *USA Today,* not many months ago, it was reported how a man got creative and tapped into the unpublished job market. As the story goes, unemployed, one early Monday morning, a man left his home in the Los Angeles area for the Los Angeles International Airport. One small detail though: He had no flight to catch. Upon arriving in the terminal in his sharpest business attire, he began to hand out his résumé to the executives standing on line to check in for their flights. One executive admired his tenacity and creative spirit so much, he called the job hunter back not many days later and offered him a job. Get active and get creative! Remember, if all the job seekers are applying through the help-wanted ads for only 15 percent of the available positions, the competition is staggering.

According to the U.S. Department of Labor, there are millions of brand-new jobs being added to the labor force each year. This means that, on an average, 65,000 to 100,000 brand-new jobs open up each week. Even if the average unemployment rate is 5 percent or as high as 9 percent in some areas, a whopping 95 percent or 91 percent of the populace has jobs. Not bad odds!

THE TOP 5 REASONS TO COLD CALL

There are many personal benefits to cold-calling:

1. You tap into a huge market of available jobs that the U.S. Department of Labor calls "unpublished."

2. You reduce your competition because the other 90 percent of the people are at home reading the want ads, competing for 15 percent of the jobs.

3. You remain current and learn of new jobs as they happen.

4. You network and gain valuable contacts that often turn into lifelong business connections that will help you in the future.

5. It helps you maintain a positive self-image as you get out daily in professional attire and remain part of the business community. (Sitting at home in your bathrobe day in and day out has a devastating effect on your self-worth.)

Here's how to cold-call. The night before you go, plan a strategy. For instance, "Tomorrow I will park my car downtown and visit every company in the World Bank Tower," or "Tomorrow I will visit all the companies at the new office park on the west side of town," or "Tomorrow I will drive to the north side of town and visit the companies located in that area."

The next day, get up early, dress in business attire, and prepare mentally just as you would for an actual interview. Arrive at your first planned location as early as 8:45 or 9:00. Bring with you fifteen to twenty résumés neatly placed in a professional-looking black folder. When you arrive at the reception area of each company, the scenario should go something like this:

First, introduce yourself: "Good morning, my name is ————." Next, state your purpose: "I don't have an appointment. However, I would like to speak with the person in charge of hiring supervisors in the customer service department. Who would that be?"

At this point, be prepared! They may contact the person in charge and you will be granted an interview on the spot, but the opposite may happen, too. They may say, "I'm sorry, that manager will not see anyone without an appointment." When this happens, you have two choices. You can politely persist. They just might sympathize with you and call the manager in to meet you. Or simply request the name or business card of that individual and leave your résumé for them. When you go home, mail them a cover letter and another résumé. Now you have achieved double name recognition.

Be aware that some companies can be very difficult to infiltrate. It would be in your best interests to call back the key decision maker and simply request a twenty-minute informative interview. This tactic very often works. Let them know you are on a mission to learn more about their influential company and not necessarily looking for a job at this time. This method helps you infiltrate the company, get your name out, make a friendly contact, and sell yourself in a subtle but effective way.

There is another way to tactfully muscle your way into

"heavily fortressed" companies. It depends on how much time you are willing to spend. There is always the volunteer route. Telephone, write, or just show up at the company. Explain you have certain skills that you are seeking to develop and/or write a paper about. Further, explain you would be willing to volunteer a certain amount of hours each week in related activities. It's free. How could they refuse?

I know of a number of people who succeeded with this tactic. Some individuals were eventually asked to stay with the company and were offered full-time positions. It seems as if everyone wants to be paid before they'll do something. But success does not always come in easy and obvious ways. Hector, for instance volunteered at the corporate office of a major international airline in New York City. And, as you may or may not know, getting a job in the corporate office of an airline without first paying your dues at the airport as a ground customer service agent or as a flight attendant is practically impossible. Initially, he worked two days a week in the office of human resources. He looked and acted as professionally and in some cases more so than the other employees in the department. He arrived at 9:00 A.M. sharp. His business attire was clean, pressed, and above average. His grooming was impeccable. Best of all, Hector's work, tasks, and assignments were executed in a timely, organized, and well-thought-out fashion. To make a long story short, after only a couple of months of volunteering, a nearby department announced a last-minute need for a new supervisor. Guess who got the job? You guessed it, Hector!

Keep in mind, as I'm sure you already have, not everyone is going to get a job offer after volunteering. Nevertheless, as a result, you will have developed new skills and will be more marketable to another organization. The company you volunteered for will also serve as an excellent reference. Often, large medical centers, government agencies, and nonprofits are eager to find individuals willing to volunteer. When your work performance is of exceptional quality in this type of situation, your career has nowhere to go but up.

Finally, upon leaving the office, thank the receptionist for her time and write her name down as well. Treat receptionists kindly, and they will become your allies. When you telephone the company, remind the receptionist who you are, and she will make sure your call gets transferred to the right person.

To help you prepare, here is a cold-calling script for you in its entirety. Practice role plays with a friend the night before. There will be minimal stage fright the next day with adequate rehearsal time. By the way, the more cold calls you make, the easier it becomes.

COLD-CALLING SCRIPT WITH FULL COOPERATION

JOB SEEKER *(to the receptionist.)*: Good morning/afternoon, my name is ——. I don't have an appointment. However, I would like to speak with the manager in charge of the —— department. Who would that be?

RECEPTIONIST: That is Ms./Mr. ——. What is this in regard to?

JOB SEEKER: Please let Ms./Mr. —— know I stopped by to ask a few questions and gain more insights into his/her department's career field. I am looking to obtain his/her advice and to investigate various companies.

RECEPTIONIST: Please wait one moment. I'll call and see if she/he is in. *(She dials the phone).* If you would, please be seated. Ms./Mr. —— will be out in a moment to see you.

JOB SEEKER: Thank you for all your help. Your name is? Thank you, ——, for everything.

(Manager comes out to lobby. Job seeker initially discusses that he/she stopped by to ask a few questions and gain more insights into the department manager's career field. Also, that he/she is looking to obtain the manager's advice and to investigate various companies. Job seeker begins to inquire about the department, advice on where to fit in, potential positions available, and if the manager would refer the job seeker to other departments and companies. A preliminary interview begins. Job seeker closes for another appointment and to pursue employment further and gets a business card.)

COLD-CALLING SCRIPT
WITH A CHALLENGE

JOB SEEKER *(to the receptionist)*: Good morning/afternoon, my name is ———— . I don't have an appointment. However, I would like to speak with the manager in charge of the ———— department. Who would that be?

RECEPTIONIST: That is Ms./Mr. ———— . What is this in regards to?

JOB SEEKER: Please let Ms./Mr. ———— know I stopped by to ask a few questions and gain more insights into his/her department's career field. I am looking to obtain his/her advice and to investigate various companies.

RECEPTIONIST: Please wait one moment. I'll call and see if she/he is in. *(she dials the phone)* I'm sorry. Ms./Mr. ———— cannot see you right now.

JOB SEEKER: I completely understand. Please leave my résumé for her/his review. By the way, do you have a business card for Ms./Mr. ———— or one for the company?

(Receptionist hands job seeker the business card.)

Thank you for all your help. Your name is? Thank you, ————, for everything.

(Job seeker exits and writes down the receptionist's name and other pertinent notes in a notebook before going on to the next call.)

The same process of cold-calling I just described to you is adapted for marketing yourself by telephone. (I call it *teleself-marketing*).

> **16** **Secure five leads per week from the Yellow Pages of the phone book or a professional business directory. Call the businesses you would like to work for and send them your résumé and cover letter.**

With teleself-marketing, you again tap into the huge market of unpublished jobs available. Just by making telephone calls, you are gathering important information and making contacts.

After you have selected a category from the Yellow Pages, begin calling. Introduce yourself just as you did on the cold call and state your purpose. Request to speak with the person in charge of hiring for your position. Try to get through to them and set up an interview, or get their name and send them a copy of your résumé and cover letter.

To help you prepare yourself, here is a teleself-marketing script for you in its entirety. As you did for cold-calling, practice with a friend the night before. With practice, you will minimize stage fright. Remember, the more phone calls you make, the easier it becomes.

TELESELF-MARKETING SCRIPT
WITH FULL COOPERATION

JOB SEEKER *(to the switchboard operator)*: Good morning/afternoon, my name is ———. The reason I am calling is to speak with the manager in charge of the ——— department. Who would that be?

SWITCHBOARD OPERATOR: Yes, that is Ms./Mr. ———. Please hold while I transfer you.

(Job Seeker is transferred to secretary in the manager's office.)

SECRETARY: Good morning/afternoon. Ms./Mr. ——'s office.

JOB SEEKER *(sounding confident)*: Good morning/afternoon, this is ——— calling. Ms./Mr. ———, please.

SECRETARY: What is this in regards to?

JOB SEEKER: Please let Ms./Mr. ——— know I'm calling to ask a few questions and gain more insights into his/her department's career field. I am looking to obtain his/her advice and to investigate various companies.

SECRETARY: Please hold one moment. Ms./Mr. ——— will be with you shortly. *(She places the job seeker on hold.)*

JOB SEEKER: Thank you very much. I'll hold.

(Manager takes the phone call. Job seeker initially discusses that he/she is calling to ask a few questions and gain more insights into the department manager's career field. Also, that he/she is looking to obtain the manager's advice and to investigate various companies. Job seeker begins to inquire about the department, advice on where to fit in, potential positions available, and if the manager would refer the job seeker to other departments and companies. Job seeker closes for an appointment to meet, touch base in person, and offers to take the manager to lunch.)

TELESELF-MARKETING SCRIPT
WITH A CHALLENGE

JOB SEEKER *(to the switchboard operator)*: Good morning/afternoon, my name is ———. The reason I am calling is to speak with the manager in charge of the ——— department. Who would that be?

SWITCHBOARD OPERATOR: Yes, that is Ms./Mr. ———. Please hold while I transfer you.

(Job seeker is transferred to secretary in the manager's office.)

SECRETARY: Good morning/afternoon. Ms./Mr. ———'s office.

JOB SEEKER *(sounding confident)*: Good morning/afternoon, this is ——— calling. Ms./Mr. ———, please.

SECRETARY: What is this in regards to?

JOB SEEKER: Please let Ms./Mr. ——— know I'm calling to ask a few questions and gain more insights into his/her department's career field. I am looking to obtain his/her advice and to investigate various companies.

SECRETARY: Please hold one moment. *(She places the job seeker on hold.)* I'm sorry, Ms./Mr. ——— is not available.

JOB SEEKER: It's very important that I speak with him/her. I can hold a moment more and see if they free up.

SECRETARY: I'm sorry. They are very busy right now.

JOB SEEKER: I understand. What would be a better time to try back? Later this morning, or this afternoon?

SECRETARY: Probably this afternoon.

JOB SEEKER: I'm sending Ms./Mr. ——— some important information. How do you spell their name and what is the address, please?

(The secretary provides the information.)

JOB SEEKER: Thank you very much for all your help. Your name is? Thank you, ———, for everything.

(The job seeker hangs up the phone and mails a résumé and cover letter to the manager. The job seeker also calls again in the afternoon and remembers to use the secretary's name.)

Highly efficient secretaries are probably the biggest obstacle when cold-calling or teleself-marketing. Please understand that they are only doing their job. Be polite and do not take it personally. However, there are ways to encourage cooperation from a secretary. One way is to sound assumptive and authoritative. If you sound important and professional (not weak or scared), in many instances you will be put right through to the manager, no questions asked. Also, you can call before or after business hours. At this time, the secretary is gone and the manager usually answers the phone. I have had tremendous cooperation from switchboard operators. Call the operator and ask authoritatively, "What's that extension for Ms./Mr. ———'s office?" or ask, "What is the direct-dial phone number for Ms./Mr. ———'s office?" Sound like you work in the building and you lost the number. It works. Get the extension, call back in, and simply ask for the number you were given.

What do you do if they ask you to leave your name and number? Don't! If you leave your name and number, they've got you. Everyone knows not to put you through when you call back. Try not to make too much notoriety. It could hinder future return calls and getting secretarial cooperation. To avoid leaving my name and number, I usually say, "Oh, no, that's okay. I'm between appointments right now. I can call back later. What would be the best time to try back?"

There is a way to double your leads when cold-calling and teleself-marketing. Here's how to do it. After you have spoken with a company representative and have established rapport, ask for a referral. Ask, "What other companies or individuals would you recommend I contact?" Most are pleased to help a job seeker and will give you names of individuals and companies, sometimes conveniently located in the same office building.

A referral has a magic all its own. When referred, you have a special entrée into a company. In most cases, the receptionist will transfer you with less questions, and the manager will be less reticent to see or speak to you.

I term a referral a *warm call*. It is a superior contact to a cold call. Generally speaking, referrals are considered prequalified leads. They have a higher potential for success than cold calls. You can ask for referrals from friends, acquaintances, relatives, and friends of friends.

As you can see, with the methods we have been discussing, when you are unemployed, you should not be wasting important business hours. Further, you can make valuable use of your evening and weekend hours by networking and attending community functions.

17 **Secure five leads through networking. Attend all job fairs, business association meetings, and community organization functions.**

Networking is the important process of getting out and attending a variety of weekly community events. Call your Chamber of Commerce. They may permit you to attend a meeting or two at no charge. The Chamber will also be able to give you the names and phone numbers of area professional associations. You can call each of them and obtain their meeting schedules.

Keep in mind that there are many professional associations that relate to your career (directly or indirectly) and they usually meet monthly. You may or may not know about them. Do some research. The local chapters will welcome your visit.

Attend your local church or synagogue and become involved in their community functions. Not only is this a good practice spiritually, but you also will have an opportunity to rub shoulders with key people in the business community.

Attend all job fairs. Job fairs have the ability to save you both time and money. You can literally meet and interview with up to 100 companies all in one place at one time. Bring plenty of résumés, dress professionally, and plan on spending the day. Take your time and network.

NETWORKING RESOURCES

Here is an expanded list of creative resources for networking and obtaining referrals.

- Professional associations

- Friends

- Relatives

- Neighbors

- On-line chat in member rooms like *America Online*

- Colleagues/coworkers

- Priest/rabbi/minister

- Teachers

- Chamber of Commerce lists

- Convention and visitor bureau lists

- University/college placement offices

- Church organizations

- Clubs

- Local political representatives

- Professionals: doctor, lawyer, banker, etc.

- Previous employment's competitors

- Employment agencies

- Exchange E-mail with professional members of an on-line service

There is a proliferation of employment agencies in all major cities.

Agencies are profit-making businesses that make their money by charging substantial fees to the employer once you are placed. But always check first. Some agencies work in reverse. They could charge you anywhere from $500 to $5,000 for a job placement. Read everything thoroughly, and be sure this is what you want to do.

In most instances, an agency takes over the responsibilities of marketing yourself for you. This may sound like the easy way out. It saves you time, frustration, and rejection, and you still get a job. However, be aware that there can be drawbacks. Realize that you might be encouraged to take a job that you normally would not have wanted. Agents work on a commission basis. Because of this, they have the unique ability to sell you on taking a particular job. You could end up in a job that will set your career back instead of forward.

I recommend utilizing agencies as only a small part of your total plan. If managed carefully, they can work effectively for you. With your own efforts and theirs, you will have more leverage when negotiating to take or not to take a job offer that they recommend.

JOB SEARCHING ON THE WEB

An electronic-based job search is an important addition to a conventional job search but should not replace it. With that said, there is an enormous compilation of sites on the World Wide Web that will help you find a job. The sites can be focused or broad. For instance, some sites are focused on the West Coast or focused in the area of engineering, and still others cover the U.S. and the world with a wide variety of job openings. Most of the sites may be found by utilizing the search engines *Infoseek, Yahoo, Lycos,* or *Excite.*

"But how do I get the job through the Internet?" you may ask. First, it is assumed that you have access to a computer, a modem, and an on-line service provider. If you don't, find out how you can (i.e., school, library, office, friend, or a commercial business center like Kinko's). For a small fee, Kinko's, which operates twenty-four hours a day in most communities, will help get you on your way to effective use of the Internet. They offer a range of complete full- and self-service options. In other words, there is no excuse *not* to expand your job search to the Internet.

One of the most well-organized and useful sites on the Web for job searching is called, *Job Search Page.* This page will lead you to other helpful sites but by no means is inclusive of all that is available. The page may be found at the following address: <*http://www.jhu.edu/~matsci/jobsearch. html* >. You may also locate the page through a search engine like *Yahoo* or *Infoseek* by entering, in quotes, "*Job Search Page*" at the search prompt. The links on this page are in no particular order other than being indexed by the type of resource (i.e., job listings, reference sources, recruiting agencies, and miscellaneous). Each link listed is maintained by independent organizations and individuals.

JOB SEARCH HOME PAGE

Although the page is constantly being updated, here is a sample of the type of information you are guaranteed to find at a Web site like the *Job Search Page.*

1. *Job listings.*

     Bio Online Career Center

     Biospace Job Server—Jobs in Biotechnology

     S. CA Job Search

     Bay Area Jobs

     SF Chronicle/Examiner Classifieds

     Andersen Consulting

     Technology Registry Employment Database

     Search Jobs in CA

     CareerMosaic

     Jobs Offered Database

     America's Job Bank Main Menu

     Online Career Center

     BioData, Inc. Job Board

     JOBS Library

     Interactive Employment Network

     Welcome to MedSearch America

Employment Opportunities and Résumé Postings

Jobs Online on the Internet

Job Jump Station

Fed Jobs in CA

WWW Classified Jobs Offered

2. *Résumé banks.* You can publish your résumé on-line for prospective employers to search through. Some are free, others are not.

Central Carolina Online Career Services: Create a profile or submit a résumé for those interested in jobs in Central Carolina Region.

Dynamic Research: Stores your on-line résumé for six months. Employers search through the résumés.

Electronic Job Match International: Résumé listing service. Employers do the searching.

The Online Career Center: Has a searchable résumé database that includes detailed instructions on how to enter your résumé into their database.

PeopleBank: Enter your résumé via an electronic form. Employers do the searching.

Résumés On-line: Provides résumé consulting, preparation, and on-line posting services.

The Résumé Publishing Company: Confidentially posts your résumé. Mainly for those who don't want to be discovered by their current employer.

Shawn's Internet Résumé Center: Gives your résumé its own home page. It also provides you with a guest book of employers who have checked you out.

Technology Registry: A résumé database devoted exclusively to the technology industries.

Interactive Employment Network

Welcome to MedSearch America: A résumé database devoted exclusively to the medical field.

Job Center

WWW Classified Résumé Post

California Career Center

Job Web: With exclusive information for new graduates.

3. *Reference sources.*

Outlook Colorado: Job opportunity newsletter

Andersen Consulting: What would it be like to work for Andersen Consulting?

NCS Career Magazine

College Grad Tips

4. *Recruiters.*

Engineering Recruiter

USA Based Recruitment Agencies

Recruiters Online Network

5. *Electronic résumés.*

   Cyberezume

   Multimedia Résumé

6. *Miscellaneous.*

   List of Newsgroups

   Career special interest groups that leave helpful tips and posts for the group or individuals
   in the group.

Besides the Internet, a job seeker has various other high-tech options for communicating with prospective employers. When used effectively, they can speed up your job search and get you a job in even less than thirty days.

Tim utilized *Get the Job You Want in Thirty Days* for his job search upon arriving in New York City not too long ago. He got a job in fourteen days using current technology to his advantage. His goal was to work in pharmaceutical sales for one of the top fifteen drug companies. Using a business directory like the *PDR (Physicians Desk Reference)*, he began calling each one of the drug companies listed in rank order in the front of the book. As he called, he used the teleself-marketing script in this chapter. Along with the standard information, he also got the hiring manager's fax number. He hung up the phone and immediately faxed a résumé and cover letter from his computer. He followed up at the end of the day by mail with original copies. Within the first four hours of faxing cover letters and résumés, he received three phone calls requesting interviews. One company saw him within a few days. He was offered a position within two weeks from the very first day of beginning his job search.

HIGH-TECH COMMUNICATION PROTOCOL

- Fax your résumé and cover letter. When you do, follow up with original copies sent the same day.

- When faxing, avoid gimmicky attention-getter cover pages.

- Don't overfax. One fax of your résumé to the same person is enough.

- Send your résumé as an E-mail attachment. Be sure you and the person who will receive the attachment have compatible programs so the résumé can be opened and read. Only do this if it has been requested by the hiring manager. Otherwise, I don't recommend it.

- Do not send a photo of yourself as an E-mail attachment.

- Use E-mail for networking purposes. Drop short messages to individuals with E-mail addresses inquiring about potential positions, referrals and advice.

- Limit your E-mails to the same person to only one or two, until the person chooses to correspond with you.

- Keep your E-mails professional and nonpersonal in content.

- Get a hiring manager's attention; send your résumé and cover letter overnight, air express, next business morning delivery.

- Scannable résumés: Most employers receive hundreds of résumés weekly and monthly. Many keep track of them in electronic databases that scan and store your résumé. For the scanner to work, keep in mind:

  Avoid graphics

  Avoid shading and shadowing

  Stapled and folded résumés do not scan well

  Bold scans well

  Type point sizes of ten to fourteen are best

  Print on one side only

  Use key nouns important to your industry and career

  Use jargon of your field

  Keep it simple

With the activities we have discussed in this chapter, you now have a clear understanding that getting a job is not a passive process that depends on luck. It can be a full-time job.

18

> **Develop leads relentlessly, include the use of the Internet. Do it daily from 9:00 to 5:00 (if you are working, on evenings and weekends). Until you achieve your goal, do not waste business hours washing your car or anything else unrelated.**

When you are serious about finding a good job quickly, do not waste precious time by performing unrelated tasks during business hours. Did you ever notice how, when looking for a job, that even cleaning the house becomes tempting? Really, be honest! Don't be a procrastinator. Take charge of your life. In the words of Denis Waitley, *The Psychology of Winning* author, "Winners make it happen! Losers let it happen!"

Let's review what we have learned in this fourth chapter:

13. Secure thirty or more leads per week.

14. Utilize the newspaper for ten leads.

15. Cold-call ten leads per week.

16. Secure five leads per week from the Yellow Pages or a professional directory.

17. Gain five leads per week through networking re-
    sources.

18. Work at lead generation relentlessly. Include the
    use of the Internet. Do not perform unrelated
    activities during business hours.

5

SELL YOURSELF AT THE INTERVIEW

The interview, no matter how you describe it, is purely a selling situation, and you are the product. After all, you are the greatest product you will ever sell.

The word *selling*, however, creates hesitation and fear in many people. Possibly you are one of them. You may have memories of yourself as a schoolchild selling candy bars door-to-door. You may subconsciously relive the rejection and the slammed doors at the mere thought of selling.

For others, the idea of selling may conjure up thoughts of men in plaid suits selling used cars that don't work. As a result of these negative images, the idea of selling yourself at an interview is repulsive and not something you would ever care to do. Reassessing one's attitude toward selling is essential to become successful at interviewing.

The fact remains that the interview is nothing more than pure selling and requires knowledge of selling techniques. Life in general is selling. We are all selling something: an idea to our children, a special date to a friend, or trying to get a seat on an airplane that is already overbooked. Here are five professional steps to selling that you should commit to memory. Implement them at an interview, and you will have the clear winning advantage over the competition.

THE FIVE STEPS TO SELF-SELLING

These five steps, in their entirety, transpire every time you interview or encounter another person. They are as follows:

Step 1—Rapport

Get the interviewer to like you within the first thirty seconds. The way to do this is to utilize rapport-builders. These are common tactics we all use to initially get others to like us. Here is a list of four rapport-builders.

1. *A sincere compliment.* You can comment on the friendly staff or even the artwork in the lobby. However, do not offer personal compliments. Avoid commenting on family photos on the desk or, if you are a gentleman, the jewelry a woman may be wearing. You could be guilty of treading in territory where you do not belong.

2. *An interest question.* Interest questions are considered ice-breakers and should not be utilized to ask personal questions. Rely on questions like, "What did you think about the last quarter of the big game last night?" or "When is the new addition of the building going to be completed?"

3. *A brief statement.* This is also considered an ice-breaker. A typical statement would be "The rain this morning was the most we've seen all year!" or "Beautiful day today. It's just like springtime again!" You can create hundreds more.

4. *Names.* As soon as possible, mention anyone you both may know or have in common. Name-dropping is always effective as a rapport-builder. It creates friendship and a sense of common ground. Name-dropping can be used at any time throughout the interview.

Step 2—Discovery

When you have an opportunity, ask discovery questions that get you exact information about what qualities they are looking for in applicants. You'll need this information later. For example, ask the interviewer, "What skills in your opinion are necessary to be successful at this position?"

Further, the purpose of the discovery stage is to find out what I call their DBM, or *dominant buying motive.* The dominant buying motive is the emotional reason why someone buys something. Research has proven that all individuals make decisions based on emotions and then rationalize their decisions with logic.

Before discussing how the DBM works in a self-selling interview situation, I would like to illustrate the point I am making with a true story from a selling situation of another sort. A gentleman walked into a hardware store and found a salesperson to help him pick out a hot water heater. Now you may ask, "What could be emotional about buying a hot water heater?" The salesperson narrowed the purchase down to one of two units. The second unit cost considerably more, but it stored twice as much hot water as the first. The salesperson began to ask good discovery questions and actually uncovered the emotional reason, that when satisfied, would motivate the customer to buy. The questioning went something like this: "How many people take showers in the morning at similar times?" The buyer said, "Four." "Who is usually the last one to take a shower?" The buyer said it was he. At this point, the salesperson began to recall the emotions of taking cold showers. "Don't you just hate it when you're the last one and the water is freezing? Especially on cold mornings! With the deluxe model, you will never be in that situation again. It may cost a little more, but you can see it is well worth it." Of course, the story ends with the buyer taking the deluxe model and the salesperson taking a large commission. Naturally, when the buyer arrives back home, he more than likely will logically explain the purchase to the family. Usually, emotions are not discussed. The logic could have been, "It was on sale," or "It was just the right dimensions to fit where the old one was." The mistake often made is to sell to logical reasons. Logic is not powerful enough to make someone act. Emotions are.

Transfer this example to a self-selling interview situation. A job seeker walks into the department manager's office for the final interview. The usual interview questions such as, "Tell me about yourself," are asked. When the opportunity arises for the job seeker to ask questions, the questions become tactful discovery questions probing to find out the manager's DBM. The exchange may sound something like this: "It appears as though you and the assistant manager put in long hours here. What are the types of things that require so much overtime?" The manager responds with honesty, "We've been working overtime constantly for

98

about six months. We just don't have enough help, and the hourly employees are limited to very few overtime hours. We often have to finish up their reports just to stay on top of things." The job seeker has now found an emotion. The department manager is overworked, stressed, and probably has very little leisure time. These are powerful, emotional situations that if addressed, should result in a job offer. The key, however, is to address them without addressing them. The job seeker responds, "I can understand how demanding a department this large can be. I am not afraid of long hours or hard work. I am most certain I can relieve some of the pressures that exist here. Within a few days, you will be able to focus on other department priorities." It would be too obvious to come out and say, "You will have more time off to be at home with your family." However, the department head will draw that emotional conclusion from what you just said. In fact, one of my students once half-jokingly said, "Give me a few weeks to settle in, and you may even find time for that weekend golf game you've been missing out on." The manager laughed and the job seeker got the job!

Step 3—Problem

Along with your discovery questions, also learn about any special problem areas or needs that may impact this position. For example, ask the interviewer, "What do you feel are the most difficult tasks associated with this position?" You already know about their general needs as indicated by the position they are looking to fill. But ask probing, open-ended questions to find out about the sensitive areas. Such sensitive areas could include details such as that previous employees disliked being asked to put in overtime, or that even though it is an accounting position, they are actually looking for someone with phone personality as well as accounting abilities. If you don't dig out these special-need areas, you will not know that they are important and that you should be selling yourself to them in the interview. Don't rely on the interviewer to automatically tell you everything that they are looking for. An interviewer may purposely omit information just to see if you demonstrate what they are looking for without prompting. Probing for these hidden problem areas will more than likely get the interviewer to talk.

Step 4—Solution

Now that you have gathered all the information necessary, begin to make statements that sell to the prospective employer's exact needs. For example, explain to the interviewer, "Earlier, you stated that computer database and word processing experience would help a prospective manager in this department gain employee trust more rapidly. Over the past years, I have taken many workshops in computer operations and will be able to learn this department's programs with little effort. I am confident with these skills I will quickly fit in as an effective manager."

The five steps established here may be best described as *solution selling*. The solution step is the process by which, as a job seeker, the interviewer is "made well." The interviewer has a need (or a problem) and it is the task of the job seeker to clearly communicate that he/she can fill that need and make the interviewer well, much in the same fashion a doctor makes a patient well.

The solution step is where you use all the information you've gathered in the previous steps to convince the interviewer that you can successfully meet the company's needs.

Step 5—Close for Action

At the end of each interview—just like the last paragraph of your cover letter—close for some type of action. Never just say, "Good-bye, thank you very much." The most reasonable close for action is to ask for the job. Simply say to the interviewer, "Based on what I have discovered here today, I'm positive that I can get immediate results in my new position. When do I start?" If the company has other requirements and interviews to be arranged, then your close for action would be to ask when you can participate in the next step. If you don't ask, don't expect a job offer.

Interviewers want you to ask for the job. If you don't ask, how will they know that you truly want to work there? Asking for the job takes place toward the end of an interview. It's similar to a salesperson who states, "I'll go to the stockroom and get you a brand-new model still in its box." The salesperson assumes you are going to buy the item.

That leads me to share with you five different ways to ask for the job. Surely one or more of them you will feel comfortable with and utilize effectively. Here are five power closes.

FIVE POWER CLOSES—ASK FOR THE JOB

1. *The alternate close.* Ask an either/or question. Example: "When would I begin employment—prior to the December holidays or after the New Year?"

2. *The misinformed close.* Ask a question that requires their correction. Example: "Did you say Judy Walker is who I would report to?" The interviewer responds, "No, it is Susan Williams." Of course you knew that, but it caused the interviewer to envision you already working for the company.

3. *The minor-point close.* Ask a question secondary to asking for the job. Example: "How many work spaces are there in the department? Would I get a work space right away, or would I be sharing?" When they answer this question, you have them visualizing you already working for the company.

4. *The assumptive close.* Make an assumptive closing statement. Example: "I'll go ahead and review my files at home and get you the system improvement analysis that you were interested in. I'll drop it off tomorrow." With being assumptive, such as this example demonstrates, you are easing yourself into the desired result without the individual having to make a yes or no decision.

   The assumptive close has as many variations as there are situations. When you are out buying something, you will notice how salespeople will often utilize the assumptive close to ease you into purchasing an item. To be truly effective in an interview, be assumptive from the minute you walk in the door. Look, act, and speak from the first minute as if you have been the one selected for the job.

5. *The creating-urgency close.* Make statements that make it urgent that they hire you. Example: "About how long will it take before you have evaluated all the candidates? I'd like to know because I have two other companies who appear to be interested. However, when given a choice, your company is clearly the best match for my skills and career."

If well-rehearsed, this tactic will send a signal to the interviewer that you are in demand. As it is with most things in life, the thing you have to compete for is the very thing you want. With the urgency close, you create urgency, competition, and demand.

Okay, now a short quiz: What are the five steps to a selling encounter? They are *rapport, discovery, problem, solution,* and *close for action.* You now have just learned the five basic steps to self-selling. When we discuss role plays, I will ask you to role-play these steps with a friend. To be effective, these five steps need to become second nature. Role-playing with a friend will help you accomplish this.

19

> **At an interview there are two ways to learn about the company: listen and ask good questions. A person who listens well and asks good questions is perceived as more intelligent than one who doesn't.**

Good listening skills are a crucial factor in interviewing successfully. With good listening skills, you are able to gather a wealth of information that will give you power. Information always gives power in any situation. Picture a rocket blasting off from its launch pad. The rocket is you. The fuel is the information you gather.

We've all been in situations where we've failed to gather enough information and have been embarrassed by our ignorance. Possibly you can remember a time when you met someone whom you thought you might like to date. Upon meeting, after only a brief discussion, you blurted out, "I hate going to the movies," or "Museums are a bore." You later find out that movies and museums are among that person's favorite things. Failure to gather information can result in failure to win friends and influence people. Listen for a while before you start blurting out what you have and how it will help the company.

Good listening is demonstrated in a number of ways. Maintain good eye contact at all times. It is not necessary to stare the person down, but don't look at the floor, either. Take notes. Note taking helps you to remember key bits of information that you will use later in the interview to sell yourself. Note taking also creates a message about you. You appear both reliable and professional. Correct body language will help you to listen. Nodding your head, leaning forward occasionally, and other gestures demonstrate you are concentrating on what the interviewer is saying.

The second way to gather information is through the art of asking questions. Formulating good questions is not as easy as it sounds. Forget everything you learned as a child about asking questions. We all learned to ask yes/no questions. Clearly, in adult communication, this kind of question gathers little information. The rocket never gets off the ground because the fuel, made of information, just isn't there.

Questions that do gather information are called *open-ended* questions. Practice these with friends and family and you will see that they actually take practice and effort to implement. Sample questions are, "Why do you feel that way?" and "What would be the best way to handle that?" and "Where do we go from here?" In general, open-ended questions are formed with *who, what, where, when, how,* and *why*. An open-ended question demands more than a one-word response. You are now on your way to getting the information you need to influence the person with whom you are speaking.

Picture this: You have a friend with whom you would like to go to the movies on Saturday. You call the friend up and ask, "Would you like to go to the movies?" You've set your friend up for a yes/no response. There are no other choices. Because of habit, most people will respond with no to this type of question. (After all, no is the first word we make extensive use of as a child.) The odds of getting a yes are considerably less. How could you call the same person and express your desire with an open-ended question? You could say, "What are your plans for the weekend? When would be a good time to go to the movies together, and what would you like to see?" The open-ended approach does not guarantee a desired response, it only increases your chances of getting a yes. Sharpen your questioning skills with the following practice sheet.

OPEN-ENDED QUESTION PRACTICE SHEET

The following is a sample list of close-ended questions (questions that may be answered with a yes or no). In the opposite column, reword the question to make it an open-ended question (one that cannot be answered with a yes or no). Remember, open-ended questions usually are formed when preceded by *who, what, where, when, how,* or *why.*

CLOSE-ENDED QUESTION	OPEN-ENDED QUESTION
Example: Can I call you Friday?	When can I call you Friday?
1. Are there advancement opportunities?	
2. Is there a training program for new hires?	
3. Do you need references?	
4. Will it take long to make your final decision?	
5. Is there an annual report available?	
6. Is there a copy of the job description?	
7. Is there time for a tour of the building?	
8. Can I see the department manager before I leave?	
9. Can I take you to lunch next week?	
10. Do you think it would be okay for me to check back with you in a few days?	

The night before your interview, prepare your wardrobe and yourself. Prepare a list of questions you will ask at the interview. A person who asks good questions is perceived as more intelligent than one who has no questions. It is appropriate to keep your questions in a black folder (the one you used for cold-calling) and read from it, if you wish, at an interview. Following is a list of questions to get you started. Add to the list questions that obviously should be asked, based on the company that has arranged the interview.

QUESTIONS YOU WILL ASK AT THE INTERVIEW

the focus of this particular y psi?
branch

1. What are the strengths of the company and the department?

2. What are the career opportunities for someone entering this position?

3. What kind of orientation and training is available to new employees?

4. What other departments will I interact with?

5. To whom would I be reporting?

6. What are the growth plans for this company and department?

How does the promotion system work?

7. What are the prospects for future promotions?

Are there going to be opportunities to
8. What opportunities are there to transfer from division to another? *work with other division?*

9. How long was my predecessor in this position? Why did he/she leave?

10. What kind of support staff is available?

11. How often will I be evaluated and when?

12. What is the continuing education and tuition reimbursement policy?

13. How would you describe the company culture? Mission? Vision? Values?

14. What is the company's management philosophy?

15. What are the expectations of the person in this position?

16. How often is overtime expected?

17. What percent of the time will be devoted to my various responsibilities?

18. What are the deadlines? Weekly? Monthly?

19. What venues do employees have to offer feedback and share creative ideas?

20. When would the position start?

Add additional questions of your own here. These questions should target precisely the company, position, and situation for which you will interview.

1. _____

2. _____

3. _____

4. _____

5. _____

6. _____

7. _____

8. _____

The night prior to your interview is the time to role-play with a family member or friend. Going to an interview without some form of rehearsal is like an actor going on stage without practicing the script. Practiced simulation prepares you to demonstrate a confident and composed attitude at the interview.

20 Use role plays to rehearse for the interview. Ask a friend to serve as the interviewer. Ask your friend to ask you questions. Your friend will pose the questions most frequently asked by interviewers.

Here is a sample list of the questions most frequently asked by interviewers. I have diagramed the list of questions so you can see a typical erroneous strategy versus a better strategy to deal with these common questions. After you read mine, you can create your own variation of the better strategy and ready your own response for role plays.

THE QUESTIONS MOST FREQUENTLY ASKED
BY INTERVIEWERS

QUESTION	ERRONEOUS STRATEGY	BETTER STRATEGY
1. Tell me about yourself.	Describe your childhood and the family pets, Goo and Buffy.	Recall incidents as far back as you would like. Incidents should demonstrate upbringing, instilled values, and a good work ethic. For example, "When I was growing up, my parents both worked. We were taught very young to help out, take responsibility, and work together."
2. Why are you leaving your last job?	"Just between you and me, my boss and I never got along since day one!"	Never—I mean, never—speak from a negative. Always speak from a positive. For example: "The department I was in admittedly had no more advancement opportunities for for years to come. I'm eager to do more with my skills."
3. Why do you want to work for us?	"I heard from a friend your company has day care and other great benefits."	"I researched the company on the Internet before I applied. It was clear it stands for quality and leadership in the industry. I believe I can help and work hard for that kind of company."
4. What do you do in your spare time?	"Watch TV."	"I have many interests. I try to work out three times a week, I read a book or two a month, and I just joined the church choir for the annual holiday play.

(*continued*)

QUESTION	ERRONEOUS STRATEGY	BETTER STRATEGY
5. What do you like about yourself?	"Uh, I don't know." (If you don't know, don't expect the interviewer to find something likeable.)	"I have a way of laughing things off. I don't take disagreements personally. I bounce back pretty fast. My friends always tell me I'm too forgiving."
6. What is one negative you want to change in yourself?	"I hate to get up in the morning. I'm not a morning person." (Guess what? You just lost the job!)	Find a negative that may also be construed as a positive. For example, "My friends say I'm like a bull in a china shop sometimes. I take charge a lot and forget to get others involved. But I'm working on it."
7. Where do you want to be two or three years from now?	"Gee I've never thought about things that far ahead. I'd just be happy with a job today."	"I'd like to be in a high-growth company with a lot of advancement opportunity. A company like yours, that when I work hard, I can prove myself ready to take the next position."
8. Why should I hire you?	"Because that's why I went to college. I know all about this." (So have the other ten candidates.)	Find something that is *uniquely* you. Something another candidate would have a difficult time competing with. For example: "The reason why you should hire me is this. I consider work a personal issue of pride. Something ingrained in me by my parents. For this reason you are assured quality work."

The erroneous strategies comments may have seemed a bit too dramatic to you, but they are replicas of similar incidents from actual interviews. An individual who employs an erroneous strategy should not be considered ignorant. It is apparent that this individual is simply not well rehearsed.

Inappropriate comments such as the ones above are often created by someone thinking off the cuff. Let's face it, the best of us have all said things we should not have when afforded no time to prepare. It is for this exact reason that our system is built around dress rehearsals, practice, and role plays. Practice! Practice! Practice!

Now you are ready to set up a role play. Before your friend arrives, make the following preparations:

1. List the questions you will ask the interviewer.

2. List the anticipated questions the interviewer will ask you.

3. List answers to the questions the interviewer will ask you.

4. Review the five steps to a selling encounter (see page 96).

When your friend arrives, give them a general introduction as to what role they are playing and what company it is they represent. Also, hand them a list of anticipated questions that will be asked of you so they can drill you.

Begin the role play with the interviewer greeting you and bringing you to their office. Your objective in the role play is to take the interviewer through the five steps of the selling encounter. Your other objective is to have clear, concise answers to the questions the interviewer will ask of you. Loosen up! Have fun and make mistakes. You'll have two left feet initially. Who cares? It's better to feel that way now than at the interview. Role play a minimum of two hours five or six times.

21 Arrive at the interview fifteen minutes early. Do not arrive late or on time.

A good candidate arrives at an interview at least fifteen minutes early. When you arrive on time, you are actually arriving late! When you arrive early, you have arrived in plenty of time to fill out important preinterview information. You also have time to watch and learn, observing the company.

22 While filling out preinterview information, sit professionally. Do not read magazines in the waiting area. Read the notes prepared for the interview.

Besides filling out preinterview information, there are many other benefits to arriving early. First, you arrive relaxed and not preoccupied with traffic and other commuter worries. You are in a better frame of mind to focus on completing a winning interview. Second, you provide yourself time to observe the company, gather valuable information, and rehearse in your mind your exact interview performance, much in the same fashion an actor rehearses lines in his mind while waiting to go on stage. Often an interviewer may ask a receptionist or employee who has observed you waiting for their opinion of you. For this reason you must recognize that you are on stage even in the waiting area.

THE DO'S AND DON'TS OF WAITING IN THE RECEPTION AREA

- Do sit professionally while waiting.

- Don't read magazines or newspapers to pass the time.

- Do review your prepared questions and interview notes.

- Do rehearse in your mind the five steps to a selling encounter.

An interviewer may or may not offer to shake hands when they approach you in the reception area. Follow their cue and only shake hands if they offer. Often an interviewer will offer a cup of coffee or soda. This is a polite and cordial gesture on their part.

23

Do not accept coffee or soda at an interview. It could weaken your position. You could spill it!

A polite refusal would sound something like this: "No thank you, I just had a cup before I arrived." From a professional standpoint, accepting coffee weakens your negotiating position at the first interview. The subliminal message is that you are being casual, familiar, and on a social call. Professionals do not want to communicate this message. Professionals want to communicate stability and a focused business attitude. Also, I have heard stories from recruiters who have actually had applicants spill the beverage all over themselves and the desk. More than likely, you will have some stage fright, so don't add more fuel to the fire. However, it is perfectly acceptable to take coffee at the final interview after an offer has been made and you're more relaxed. This gesture denotes, on a subliminal level, that you integrate easily and are a welcomed new member to the team.

24

Do not discuss exact salary amounts at the first interview. Leave the salary open and discuss details after an offer has been made, probably at the final interview.

In most circumstances, you should not discuss salary at the first interview. The interviewer will make it a point to ask you your salary requirements. If it is the first interview, always respond, "Open." Countless individuals have lost job opportunities by answering this question with an exact amount.

Odds are, if you state a figure that is too high, you will appear demanding and overrated. Conversely, if you state a figure that is too low, you'll be perceived as a poor performer.

After you state that your salary requirements are open, explain to the interviewer that you have come to the interview with an open mind. Explain further that you believe that the right position with the right benefits would make your salary very negotiable.

Don't make the mistake of going to the first interview and making salary/compensation demands. It shouldn't even be discussed. It is assumed that you would not have gone to the interview if you did not feel the position would at least be in the ballpark of your compensation requirements. Discussion of salary and compensation requirements come at the final interview, after a job offer has been made. At this point, it has been determined that they want you. What a great feeling it is to be wanted! Now you are in a better position to negotiate.

What if they blurt out an objection during an interview? A typical objection may be stated as, "You seem like you don't have enough experience," or "We were looking for someone a bit more diverse in their background." What should you do? The first thing to do is relax. See objections as a positive experience. Rejoice when you hear an objection. It means that the interviewer is thinking and trying to give you full consideration. I would be leery of any interviewer who does not have an objection. If they have no objections, it more than likely means they are not interested in you at all.

THE FOUR TIMES TO HANDLE AN OBJECTION

There are four times when it is appropriate to handle an objection in an interview. They are:

1. *Before they ask.* The night before the interview, you should make a list of the most obvious objections that might come up in the interview. Be ready for the obvious and even bring it up before they ask. For example, if you truly don't have years of experience and you know it's going to come up, attack it head on. They will respect you for it. Say, "I know I don't have five to ten years of experience like some, but I do have an open-minded will-learn-anything attitude. I don't stop working until I achieve satisfactory results."

2. *When they ask.* Again, preparation the night before in your role plays will help you come off sounding confident and smooth. You can really impress the interviewer by sounding like you welcome adversity. After all, problem solving is considered a respected quality in business professionals. Once the objection is stated, you respond with, "I'm glad you asked that!" or "That's a good question." Then proceed to give your explanation.

3. *Later.* It may not be appropriate in your mind to handle the objection right when it is asked. The interviewer will understand as long as you have a good reason for putting off an answer. For instance, the objection could be, "I don't think we have the budget available to hire someone at your level of experience. You appear to be overqualified." You could respond with, "The important thing is that you feel comfortable with my abilities. We can discuss compensation later. I'm sure we can work out something mutually agreeable."

4. *Never.* This situation in objection-handling is rare, but it is appropriate for certain instances. Usually, it works best with objections that are minor, such as, "It sure sounds like you are qualified; however, it would be even better if you knew how to operate WordPerfect on a PC instead of Microsoft Word." You intentionally dust the objection under the carpet so as not to make a mountain out of a molehill. Simply continue to sell yourself and draw attention to the universality of all word processing programs. There could be no reason to split hairs over this type of issue.

Practice! Practice! Practice! Come home from an interview and write down the objections you may have mishandled, a question you know you did not have a reasonable answer to. Then practice handling the objections with well-thought-out, prepared answers in a mirror or with a friend.

The worst thing to do when hearing an objection is to argue. Take, for instance, the objection, "You appear to be overqualified and out of our salary range." A person easily could become indignant and say, "You're a big company. You should be able to afford quality when you find it." Guess what? This person just lost the job. Don't argue about anything in an interview. The interviewer is always right. One company I worked for purposely instructed interviewers to create objections and to cause friction at interviews. You can take issue with anything you want. However, you might win the battle but lose the war.

Here is a simple but effective four-step method to objection-handling. You can remember it by memorizing LAER. *L* stands for *listen*. Leaning forward when you hear an objection and having eye contact demonstrates you are confident and would make a good employee. *A* stands for *acknowledge*. Repeat back in paraphrase form the objection you just heard. This tells the interviewer you were listening and that you understand the question. It also clarifies the question. It would be embarrassing to have misunderstood the question. *E* stands for *explore*. Ask an open-ended question such as, "Tell me more about why you feel that way," or "Why do you ask that?" The explore stage helps you to gather more information about the objection. Always remember in any negotiations that the more information you have, the more power you have. Finally, *R* stands for *respond*. You now have completed enough preliminaries to respond effectively. Unfortunately, many individuals go right from the objection to a responce. They miss all the middle steps. Can you see how much more effective you are when you include the other steps?

In summary, the interview is a selling situation. The one who sells the hardest and best wins. Remember, you are the greatest product you will ever sell.

Let's review now what we've learned in this chapter:

19. Before the interview, prepare. Compile a list of questions you will ask the recruiter.

20. Role-play with a friend the five steps to a selling encounter and rehearse the questions you will ask the interviewer as well as the questions you will be asked.

21. Arrive at the interview fifteen minutes early.

22. Be professional as you wait in the reception area.

23. Do not accept coffee or soda at an interview.

24. Do not discuss salary at the first interview.

6

FOLLOW UP
RELENTLESSLY

Upon arriving home after your interview, feeling a bit relieved and elated that it's all over, you still have work to do—work that when performed properly will keep your name ahead of the competition long after the interview has passed. With follow-up, you're on the home stretch to getting a job in thirty days. Effective follow-up requires a delicate, tactful technique. Begin with sending a thank-you note.

25
> **Send a handwritten thank-you note to the interviewer. Thank the interviewer for their time and consideration.**

Let's be optimistic and assume that you will be getting many interviews over the next month. This would be a good time for you to go out to a stationery store and purchase a small box of very plain and simple thank-you notes. Avoid the types with birds and flowers. Keep it simple!

After each interview, send a handwritten thank-you note to the interviewer if it is short in length. It is appropriate to send a computer generated letter if it is long in length similar to the one on the next page. However, you have already generated your résumé and cover letter by computer. That was a high-tech presentation. Handwriting a thank-you note is high-touch. It adds some personal warmth to your style. Also, it indicates sincerity and attention to detail. It's another chance to sell some good qualities about yourself.

THANK-YOU LETTER TIPS

A good thank-you letter should contain the following elements:

- Express appreciation for the interviewer's time and consideration.

- Reconfirm your interest in the position.

- Confirm your understanding of the next step.

- Enclose any new information or developments that may help you get hired.

- If necessary, nudge the employer into a decision by indicating that another employer is pressing and a decision to possibly hire you is imminent.

SAMPLE THANK-YOU LETTER

Date of letter

Your name
Street Address
City, State, Zip

Dear Mr./Ms.,

Thank you very much for your time, consideration, and giving me the opportunity to interview with you on (day). Upon leaving your office, I had considerable time to reflect upon on our discussion. I am convinced now more than ever that working at (company name) is where I can really make a difference with my talents and abilities.

I am sending under separate cover, a copy of the project that I wrote and we discussed at the interview. We can speak later, after you have had a chance to read it as to how it can be used in my new position.

From what I understand you need to review my application with the department manager before getting back to me. I look forward to hearing from you at your earliest possible convenience as another employer may be extending an offer soon. However, I would most prefer to make a commitment to (company) once your decision to hire me has been made. When can we finalize the details? I may be reached at (phone number).

Sincerely,

Your handwritten name
Your typed name

Without being obtrusive, call the interviewer once or twice after the interview and after your thank-you note has arrived. Don't be horrified by the thought of doing this.

---

26 **Call the interviewer once or twice after the interview. When you sense a high level of interest, follow up again.**

Follow-up can work in your favor if you use this simple formula. First, state a valid purpose for making the follow-up call. The worst thing to do is to call and ask, "How are things going with my job application?" The better approach would be to say, "The reason why I am calling is to find out what additional information you might need in order to complete my application file." Second, thank them again for their time and consideration and ask when they anticipate getting back to you with a potential job offer.

The main purpose of this type of follow-up is to take what I call "a temperature check." If they appear to be cold and indifferent, go on to other priorities. If they appear to be warm and enthusiastic, consider it a hot prospect and plan other forms of follow-up until you get a job offer. An additional form of follow-up I have used successfully for my hot prospects is stopping by their office a week or two after the interview. This tactic may sound pushy to you, but it really isn't as long as it's done properly. If they are at all interested in you, they will respect you for the effort.

126

Before calling, check your telephone skills. Always smile when speaking on the telephone. Many large telephone operations such as airline reservation rooms require mirrors in front of the operators. Smiling forces your voice to imply that your are an energetic and responsible person. Generally speaking, research has proven that people who smile have higher credibility.

Now you're ready to call. Here's how to do it. Telephone the interviewer and state that tomorrow you will be in their neighborhood and would like to stop by for a moment. Explain you have some new letters of reference or copies of previous projects you have worked on that you would like to share with them and add to your application file. If they are at all interested in you, they will welcome this new information. Just make sure you have substantial, new information to bring. That's why, when at all possible, hold a few things back from the interview so you can use them later as a reason to visit and follow up.

Arrive at their office at the designated time and be sure you have with you exactly what you promised to bring. At the end of your time together, close for action by asking for the job. If an offer is not extended, determine what is the next step in the hiring process.

When I interviewed with one manager many years ago, I actually utilized this tactic three times. It worked. I was determined to get the job. Over a period of two months, I stopped by three times and asked for the job at the end of each session. At the second session, he invited his boss in to meet me. They both asked in unison before showing me the door, "Do you have any further questions?" "Yes," I replied politely, "when do I start?" Truly, I must admit, I noticed shock in their eyes. It appeared that it was the last question they expected! They both grinned and said, "We'll see, let's stay in touch." I may not have received a job offer that very day, but I do believe that my ability to remain persistent and ask for the job earned me an offer not many days later.

27 **Love the word no. Learn to love rejection. The more no's, the closer you are to yes. It only takes one yes.**

As we discussed in chapter 4, learn to love the word no. We also reviewed making a commitment to accelerate the number of no's you are going to get. The reason, you realize, is that for every no you get, you are one step closer to a yes. Always remember the illustration of the casino and numbers game. All you need is one yes. The odds are in your favor.

But how far do you go in following up? Is there a point when one should just simply move on? In answer to those questions, I'll share a short true story and you draw your own conclusion. A few years ago, I responded to a recruitment display ad in the *Miami Herald*. A few weeks later, I received the standard rejection letter. You know the one, "I am sorry, although your qualifications are impressive, we have hired someone with a more suitable background for the position," etc., etc. Now, most individuals would normally take that kind of letter as the gospel truth, file it in the trash, and move on. I didn't. I was not going to take no for an answer. My internal self-talk was, "I want to work for you, and you're going to hire me." I immediately drafted a letter to the director of human resources. First, I thanked the director for updating me regarding my application. Next, I went back to selling myself. I created a paragraph giving the reader alternate ideas, based on my résumé, as to where I might fit into a position with their company. Last, I closed for action by asking, "when can we meet to discuss the available opportunities further?" I enclosed an expanded three-page version of my one-page résumé, which they had not received from my response to the *Miami Herald* display ad. Within a week of mailing the letter, I was contacted by the director's assistant. I was on a plane to New York City for a job interview with their company that same week. Within a month, I was employed in their corporate office with my own office overlooking New York's Fifth Avenue. When do you quit following up? You be the judge.

Be forewarned not to oversell after a job offer has been made. Learn to shut up! You could talk yourself out of a job. Stop selling once you've been offered the position. At this point, focus your energy on negotiating salary, benefits, and start date.

28 When a job offer comes, learn to shut up! Don't oversell. Accept all positions offered to you. Think it over at home. Don't burn bridges in an interview.

This is a perfect time to discuss that it is in your best interest to initially accept all positions offered to you. Always say yes, even if the terms are not totally agreeable to you. The place to make your final decision is at home with family and in the peace of your own mind. If, after thinking about it, you do not want the position, you can always call and decline or even ask to renegotiate terms. If they want you badly enough, they will negotiate. Don't burn any bridges in an interview.

29 **Be flexible. A position with less income but great potential is often the best bet to get your foot in the door. What seems to be short-term loss could actually have long-term gain.**

Being flexible once a job offer has been made is very important. The ideal situation may not exist. A position with initially less income but great advancement potential is often the best bet to get your foot in the door. With a good company, you are embarking on the start of a solid career. Remember, what appears to be short-term loss actually has long-term gain.

ACCEPTING AN OFFER

After receiving an offer and after you have given a verbal acknowledgment, a written acknowledgment should be made as well. Send your letter once you receive their letter of employment. Your acceptance letter is not a legal contract but a written statement of the position as you understand the offer to be. Include in the letter such items as date and time of physical examination (if required), first day of work, position, title, reporting manager, and compensation.

SAMPLE LETTER ACCEPTING AN OFFER

Name
Street Address
City, State, Zip

Date of letter

Name
Title
Company
Street Address
City, State, Zip

Dear Mr./Ms.: ———

I am pleased to accept your invitation to take the position of (job title) for (company) at the monthly salary of $———. My reporting relationship will be to (immediate manager's name). I understand I am to have an employment physical examination on (day, date, time) at (company name and location). Thank you for this opportunity to be a member of your team.

As advised in your letter of employment, I will report to your office at 9:00 on (date). I look forward to my future association with (company), not only meeting but exceeding the company's expectations in this position.

Yours truly,

(Handwritten signature)

Your name, typed

REJECTING AN OFFER

Because you have embarked on an aggressive thirty-day job search, it is likely that you will have received more than one job offer. As soon as you have chosen to work for a particular company, notify all other employers of your decision. In your letter, thank them for their interest, explain that it was a difficult decision to make, and that another opportunity better fit your current interests and requirements. Don't burn any bridges. Make a statement keeping the door open in the future. You may need it. It is not necessary to give the exact name of the company you ultimately selected.

SAMPLE LETTER REJECTING AN OFFER

Name
Street Address
City, State, Zip

Date of letter

Name
Title
Company
Street Address
City, State, Zip

Dear Mr./Ms.: ———

Thank you for your employment offer for the position of (job title) with (company). Recently, I accepted a similar position with another company and I am unable to accept your offer at this time.

This has been a difficult decision to make. However, I look forward to the possibility of our paths crossing again in the future. Thank you for the opportunity to have had an interview and discuss career possibilities with your company.

Yours truly,

(Handwritten signature)

Your name, typed

30

> **Rely on this book's activity planner. There is no such thing as good luck. Rely totally on a good plan and good selling, and you will achieve your goal.**

Immediately following is a thirty-day activity planner designed to go with this proven system. The daily activity monitored in this plan is what makes you successful in the job search process. It is the very difference that makes this job search you are embarking on more successful and a more positive experience than others you have embarked upon in the past.

Faithfully perform the activities and fill out this plan for the next thirty days. Commit yourself to the effort described in the plan. Be relentless and determined to achieve your goal. With your determination and this plan, you will definitely come out a winner. In fact, you are a winner now if you believe it.

Let's review what we have learned in this chapter:

25. Send a thank-you note.

26. Call the interviewer once or twice after the interview, but have a reason.

27. Remember the more no's you get, the closer you are to a yes.

28. Don't oversell. Learn to shut up!

29. Be flexible.

30. Do not rely on luck. Rely on this book's activity planner.

7

THE ACTIVITY
PLANNER

Why use an activity planner? Isn't just reading this book enough? Simply stated, no. Information that is not put into action remains simply that, information. The activity planner is what makes this job search system effective. It is the only book of its kind that monitors key, critical job search activities on a daily basis. This book and the activity planner are the only job search tools you will ever need.

The activity planner will provide you with a concise synopsis of this entire book. You will notice that each day features a corresponding key concept.

During the thirty-day process, you will discover new ways to refine the key concepts and tailor them to your needs. Again, you will become aware of the main ideas as you see them listed on a daily basis.

This action plan provides you with two attack options. The first is to work diligently five days a week for thirty days. The second is to work nonstop seven days a week for thirty days. Deciding to work on your plan five days a week provides you at the end of thirty days with 120 contacts. However, for those of you with the time, to assure even greater success, I recommend pursuing the thirty-day-straight option. Here, you receive a total of 180 leads. Should you decide on this option, fill in the pages marked Bonus Days, to represent weekends. The difference between 120 and 180 could mean having or not having more than one offer to choose from. Commit yourself to the extra work if you can afford the time.

This action plan also requires registering your résumé with as many of the Internet's on-line résumé databases as possible, as it is explained in chapter 4. The action plan also requires that you take the time to search on-line employer databases and send them your electronic résumé or profile. The electronic job search is a required bonus activity in order to diversify your job search and add extra insurance to getting a job offer within thirty days. However important these activities are, it does not replace the day-to-day conventional activities also outlined in this plan.

Be aware that day one represents a Monday. Begin your action plan on a Monday, when you are fresh and a new business week has begun. Also, it will keep in line the bonus days as weekends, should you decide to increase the quantity and quality of your success.

The activity planner is a step-by-step action plan that, when diligently followed, will get you a job in thirty days or less. Follow closely the steps listed here and fully complete the activity planner. The activity planner must be completed on a daily basis to assure that you are putting the proper amount of work and strategy into your job search. Remember, do not rely on good luck. Rely on a good plan—the activity planner.

CHECK ATTITUDE

Today I practiced positive self-talk and visualization (check one).

———   Positive all day

———   Positive only part of the day

———   Doubtful and negative most of the day

CHECK LEAD GENERATION

I discovered six new hot leads today (list below)

COMPANY NAME   CONTACT

1. _____

2. _____

3. _____

4. _____

5. _____

6. _____

CHECK RÉSUMÉ AND COVER LETTER

I sent résumés and cover letters to all six new hot leads (list below).

COMPANY NAME   CONTACT   ADDRESS   PHONE   E-MAIL

1. _____

2. _____

3. _____

4. _____

5. _____

6. _____

CHECK INTERVIEW

I practiced interview role-plays with a friend (list interviews).

COMPANY NAME CONTACT DATE/TIME ADDRESS PHONE E-MAIL

1. _____

2. _____

3. _____

CHECK THANK-YOU NOTE FOLLOW-UP

Thank you notes sent? Yes _____ No_____

COMPANY NAME   CONTACT   ADDRESS   PHONE   E-MAIL

1. _____

2. _____

3. _____

CHECK PHONE CALLS FOLLOW-UP

Follow-up phone calls made? Yes_____ No_____

COMPANY NAME   CONTACT   ADDRESS   PHONE   E-MAIL

1. _____

2. _____

3. _____

CHECK INTERNET RÉSUMÉ REGISTRATION

Today, I registered my résumé with at least one on-line résumé service.

SERVICE'S NAME   INTERNET ADDRESS   OTHER INFORMATION

1. _____

2. _____

3. _____

CHECK INTERNET EMPLOYER DATABASES

Today, I searched employer databases and sent at least three electronic résumés or profiles to prospective employers.

COMPANY NAME   INTERNET ADDRESS   OTHER INFORMATION

1. _____

2. _____

3. _____

WEEK ONE

Day One

> 1
>
> **If you think you can't, you won't. If you think you can you will!**

Day Two

> 2
>
> **Practice positive self-talk: "I can! I will! I know I can do it!"**

Day Three

> 3
>
> **Neutralize negative self-talk ("I'm worried. What if I don't get the job?") with positive, winning statements.**

Day Four

4 **Don't blame others. Take responsibility for yourself and your career. Don't blame previous jobs, bosses, or even your family for your current situation.**

Day Five

5 **Practice visualization. When you lie awake in the morning or evening, visualize already working at and enjoying the career you want.**

Bonus Day Six

6

> Dress like a winner. Make sure your
> clothes are clean and pressed. Make sure
> your hair and image are clean and sim-
> ple.

Bonus Day Seven

7

> Design a one-page résumé. Give just
> enough information to prompt an inter-
> view. Leave the reader wanting more.

WEEK TWO

Day Eight

8 Print out your résumé on white paper only, using a professional résumé computer software template. Use spell check and make sure that your grammar is correct.

Day Nine

9 Utilize action words constantly throughout the résumé. Take the time to be creative; use a thesaurus to avoid duplication of action words.

Day Ten

10 Target the résumé to each particular company and position.

Day Eleven

11

A cover letter has three distinct paragraphs.

1. *Attention.* The first paragraph gets the reader's attention with important facts or features about you.

2. *Benefit.* The second paragraph tells the company the benefits of hiring you.

3. *Close for action.* The last paragraph must close for the interview. Simply state, "When can an interview be arranged? I can be reached at [give your telephone number]."

Day Twelve

12

The purpose of the résumé and cover letter is to get you the interview. Even the best résumé and cover letter is not likely to result in a job offer. Most companies do not hire sight unseen. The interview is where you sell yourself and get the job.

Bonus Day Thirteen

13

Secure six new leads a day (thirty a week) and send them your cover letter and résumé. (Boxes 14, 15, and 16 explain where to find new leads.)

Bonus Day Fourteen

14

Secure ten leads a week from the newspaper's help wanted section. Send your cover letter and résumé.

WEEK THREE

Day Fifteen

15 Secure ten leads a week from cold calls. Simply drop in on ten businesses, leave a résumé, and get the name of the person who hires for your position. Go back home and mail them a cover letter and résumé. Better yet, try to see them while you are there.

Day Sixteen

16 Secure five leads per week from the yellow pages of the phone book or a professional business directory. Call the businesses you would like to work for and send them your résumé and cover letter.

Day Seventeen

17 Secure five leads through networking. Attend all job fairs, business association meetings, and community organization functions.

Day Eighteen

18 Develop leads relentlessly. Include the use of the internet. Do it daily from 9:00 to 5:00 (if you are working, on evenings and weekends). Until you achieve your goal, do not waste business hours washing your car or anything else unrelated.

Day Nineteen

19 At an interview there are two ways to learn about the company: listen and ask good questions. A person who listens well and asks good questions is perceived as more intelligent than one who doesn't.

Bonus Day Twenty

20 Use role plays to rehearse for the interview. Ask a friend to serve as the interviewer. Ask your friend questions. Your friend will pose the questions most frequently asked by interviewers.

Bonus Day Twenty-one

21 Arrive at the interview fifteen minutes early. Do not arrive late or on time.

Day Twenty-two

While filling out preinterview information, sit professionally. Do not read magazines in the waiting area. Read the notes prepared for the interview.

Day Twenty-three

Do not accept coffee or soda at an interview. It could weaken your position. You could spill it!

Day Twenty-four

Do not discuss exact salary amounts at the first interview. Leave the salary open and discuss details after an offer has been made, probably at the final interview.

Day Twenty-five

25 Send a handwritten thank-you note to the interviewer. Thank the interviewer for their time and consideration.

Day Twenty-six

26 Call the interviewer once or twice after the interview. When you sense a high level of interest, follow up again.

Bonus Day Twenty-seven

27 Love the word no. Learn to love rejection. The more no's, the closer you are to a yes. It only takes one yes.

Bonus Day Twenty-eight

28

> When a job offer comes, learn to shut up! Don't oversell. Accept all positions offered to you. Think it over at home. Don't burn bridges in an interview.

WEEK FIVE

Day Twenty-nine

29 **Be flexible. A position with less income but great potential is often the best bet to get your foot in the door. What seems to be short-term loss could actually have long-term gain.**

Day Thirty

30 **Rely on this book's activity planner. There is no such thing as good luck. Rely totally on a good plan and good selling, and you will achieve your goal.**

CORRESPOND WITH THE
AUTHOR DIRECTLY
ON THE INTERNET

Mr. Grappo appreciates hearing from readers of his books and participants in his seminars. Write when you have an experience to share. Success stories based on the use of his concepts are always welcome. Also, to order quantities of his books or to reach the author for a speaking engagement, E-mail him at the following address: <gjgjoseph@aol.com>

Other books by Gary Joseph Grappo are available for review and purchase on the Internet at <www.Amazon.com>

BIBLIOGRAPHY

Bolles, Richard Nelson. *The 1996 What Color Is Your Parachute?* Berkeley: Ten Speed Press, 1996.

Carnegie, Dale. *How to Stop Worrying and Start Living.* New York: Simon & Schuster, 1944, 1985.

The Catalyst Staff. *Marketing Yourself.* New York: Putnam Publishing, 1980–86.

Elsea, Janet G. *The Four Minute Sell.* New York: Simon & Schuster, 1984.

Gawain, Shakti. *Creative Visualization.* New York: Bantam Books, 1995.

Grappo, Gary Joseph. *The Top 10 Fears of Job Seekers.* New York: Berkley Books, 1996.

———. *How to Write Better Résumés.* New York: Barron's, 1994.

————. *The Top 10 Career Strategies for Making a Living in the Year 2000 and Beyond.* New York: Berkley Books, 1997.

Helmstetter, Shad. *What to Say When You Talk to Yourself.* New York: Simon & Schuster, 1986.

Hill, Napoleon. *Think and Grow Rich.* New York: Fawcett Crest, 1988.

Hopkins, Tom. *How to Master the Art of Selling.* New York: Warner Books, 1982.

Jackson, Carole. *Color for Men.* New York: Ballantine Books, 1987.

————. *Color Me Beautiful.* New York: Random House, Inc., 1987.

Jackson, Tom. *Guerrilla Tactics in the Job Market.* New York: Bantam Books, 1978.

Kennedy, Lain Joyce. *Electronic Job Search Revolution.* New York: John Wiley & Sons, Inc., 1995.

————. *Electronic Résumé Revolution.* New York: John Wiley & Sons, Inc., 1996.

Sinetar, Marsha. *Do What You Love, the Money Will Follow.* New York: Dell, 1989.

Tracy, Brian. *The Science of Self-Confidence* (tape series). Solana Beach, CA: Brian Tracy, 1990.

Waitley, Denis. *The Psychology of Winning.* New York: Berkley Books, 1986.